NATIONAL INCIDENT MANAGEMENT SYSTEM

December 2008

Homeland
Security

Homeland
Security

December 18, 2008

Dear NIMS Stakeholders:

Homeland Security Presidential Directive (HSPD)-5, *Management of Domestic Incidents*, directed the development and administration of the National Incident Management System (NIMS). Originally issued on March 1, 2004, by the Department of Homeland Security (DHS), NIMS provides a consistent nationwide template to enable Federal, State[1], tribal, and local[2] governments, nongovernmental organizations (NGOs), and the private sector to work together to prevent, protect against, respond to, recover from, and mitigate the effects of incidents, regardless of cause, size, location, or complexity.

HSPD-5 also required DHS to establish a mechanism for ongoing coordination to provide strategic direction for, and oversight of, NIMS. The National Integration Center's (NIC) Incident Management Systems Integration Division (IMSI)—formerly the NIMS Integration Center—was established to support both routine maintenance and the continuous refinement of NIMS.

Since 2006, the NIMS document has been revised to incorporate best practices and lessons learned from recent incidents. The NIMS revision also clarifies concepts and principles, and refines processes and terminology throughout the document. A wide range of feedback was incorporated while maintaining the core concepts of NIMS and no major policy changes were made to the document during the revision. Below is a summary of changes to the NIMS document:

- Eliminated redundancy;
- Reorganized document to emphasize that NIMS is more than the Incident Command System (ICS);
- Clarified ICS concepts;
- Increased emphasis on planning and added guidance on mutual aid;
- Clarified roles of private sector, NGOs, and chief elected and appointed officials;

---

[1] As defined in the Homeland Security Act of 2002 P.L.107-296, the term "State" means any State of the United States, the District of Columbia, the Commonwealth of Puerto Rico, Guam, American Samoa, the Commonwealth of the Northern Mariana Islands, and any possession of the United States." 6 U.S.C. 101 (14)

[2] As defined in the Homeland Security Act of 2002, Section 2(10); the term "local government" means "(A) county, municipality, city, town, township, local public authority, school district, special district, intrastate district, council of governments... regional or interstate government entity, or agency or instrumentality of a local government; an Indian tribe or authorized tribal organization, or in Alaska a Native village or Alaska Regional Native Corporation; and a rural community, unincorporated town or village, or other public entity." 6 U.S.C. 101(10)

- Expanded the Intelligence/Investigation function; and
- Highlighted relationship between NIMS and National Response Framework.

I ask for your continued assistance as we implement NIMS. I look forward to continuing our collective efforts to better secure the homeland and protect our citizens. Thank you for your hard work in this important endeavor.

Sincerely,

Michael Chertoff

CONTENTS

LIST OF TABLES

LIST OF FIGURES

What Is the National Incident Management System?

The *National Incident Management System* (NIMS) provides a systematic, proactive approach to guide departments and agencies at all levels of government, nongovernmental organizations, and the private sector to work seamlessly to prevent, protect against, respond to, recover from, and mitigate the effects of incidents, regardless of cause, size, location, or complexity, in order to reduce the loss of life and property and harm to the environment. NIMS works hand in hand with the *National Response Framework* (NRF). NIMS provides the template for the management of incidents, while the NRF provides the structure and mechanisms for national-level policy for incident management.

PREFACE

On February 28, 2003, the President issued Homeland Security Presidential Directive 5 (HSPD–5), "Management of Domestic Incidents," which directed the Secretary of Homeland Security to develop and administer a *National Incident Management System* (NIMS). This system provides a consistent nationwide template to enable Federal, State, tribal, and local governments, nongovernmental organizations (NGOs), and the private sector to work together to prevent, protect against, respond to, recover from, and mitigate the effects of incidents, regardless of cause, size, location, or complexity. This consistency provides the foundation for utilization of NIMS for all incidents, ranging from daily occurrences to incidents requiring a coordinated Federal response.

NIMS is not an operational incident management or resource allocation plan. NIMS represents a core set of doctrines, concepts, principles, terminology, and organizational processes that enables effective, efficient, and collaborative incident management.

HSPD–5 also required the Secretary of Homeland Security to develop the *National Response Plan*, which has been superseded by the *National Response Framework* (NRF). The NRF is a guide to how the Nation conducts all-hazards response. The NRF identifies the key principles, as well as the roles and structures, that organize national response. In addition, it describes special circumstances where the Federal Government exercises a larger role, including incidents where Federal interests are involved and catastrophic incidents where a State would require significant support.

HSPD–5 requires all Federal departments and agencies to adopt NIMS and to use it in their individual incident management programs and activities, as well as in support of all actions taken to assist State, tribal, and local governments. The directive requires Federal departments and agencies to make adoption of NIMS by State, tribal, and local organizations a condition for Federal preparedness assistance (through grants, contracts, and other activities). NIMS recognizes the role that NGOs and the private sector have in preparedness and activities to prevent, protect against, respond to, recover from, and mitigate the effects of incidents.

Building on the foundation provided by existing emergency management and incident response systems used by jurisdictions, organizations, and functional disciplines at all levels, NIMS integrates best practices into a comprehensive framework for use nationwide by emergency management/response personnel[1] in an all-hazards context. These best practices lay the groundwork for the components of NIMS and provide the mechanisms for the further development and refinement of supporting national standards, guidelines, protocols, systems, and technologies. NIMS fosters the development of specialized technologies that facilitate emergency management and incident response activities, and allows for the adoption of new approaches that will enable continuous refinement of the system over time.

The Secretary of Homeland Security, through the National Integration Center (NIC), Incident Management Systems Integration Division (formerly known as the NIMS Integration Center), publishes the standards, guidelines, and compliance protocols for determining whether a Federal, State, tribal, or local government has implemented NIMS.

---

[1] Emergency management/response personnel include Federal, State, territorial, tribal, substate regional, and local governments, nongovernmental organizations, private-sector organizations, critical infrastructure owners and operators, and all other organizations and individuals who assume an emergency management role.

PREFACE

Additionally, the Secretary, through the NIC, manages publication and collaboratively, with other departments and agencies, develops standards, guidelines, compliance procedures, and protocols for all aspects of NIMS.

This document was developed through a collaborative intergovernmental partnership with significant input from the incident management functional disciplines, NGOs, and the private sector. Originally published on March 1, 2004, the document was revised in 2008 to reflect contributions from stakeholders and lessons learned during recent incidents.

INTRODUCTION AND OVERVIEW

A. INTRODUCTION

The September 11, 2001, terrorist attacks and the 2004 and 2005 hurricane seasons highlighted the need to focus on improving emergency management, incident response capabilities, and coordination processes across the country. A comprehensive national approach, applicable at all jurisdictional levels and across functional disciplines, improves the effectiveness of emergency management/response personnel[2] across the full spectrum of potential incidents and hazard scenarios (including but not limited to natural hazards, terrorist activities, and other manmade disasters). Such an approach improves coordination and cooperation between public and private agencies/organizations in a variety of emergency management and incident response activities. The *National Incident Management System* (NIMS) framework sets forth the comprehensive national approach (see Table 1).

Incidents typically begin and end locally, and are managed on a daily basis at the lowest possible geographical, organizational, and jurisdictional level. However, there are instances in which successful incident management operations depend on the involvement of multiple jurisdictions, levels of government, functional agencies, and/or emergency responder disciplines. These instances require effective and efficient coordination across this broad spectrum of organizations and activities.

NIMS uses a systematic approach to integrate the best existing processes and methods into a unified national framework for incident management. Incident management refers to how incidents are managed across all homeland security activities, including prevention, protection, and response, mitigation, and recovery.

This framework forms the basis for interoperability and compatibility that will, in turn, enable a diverse set of public and private organizations to conduct well-integrated and effective emergency management and incident response operations. Emergency management is the coordination and integration of all activities necessary to build, sustain, and improve the capability to prepare for, protect against, respond to, recover from, or mitigate against threatened or actual natural disasters, acts of terrorism, or other manmade disasters. It does this through a core set of concepts, principles, procedures, organizational processes, terminology, and standard requirements applicable to a broad community of NIMS users.

---

[2] Emergency management/response personnel include Federal, State, territorial, tribal, substate regional, and local governments, nongovernmental organizations, private-sector organizations, critical infrastructure owners and operators, and all other organizations and individuals who assume an emergency management role.

Table 1. Overview of NIMS

What NIMS Is:	What NIMS Is NOT:
• A comprehensive, nationwide, systematic approach to incident management, including the Incident Command System, Multiagency Coordination Systems, and Public Information • A set of preparedness concepts and principles for all hazards • Essential principles for a common operating picture and interoperability of communications and information management • Standardized resource management procedures that enable coordination among different jurisdictions or organizations • Scalable, so it may be used for all incidents (from day-to-day to large-scale) • A dynamic system that promotes ongoing management and maintenance	• A response plan • Only used during large-scale incidents • A communications plan • Only applicable to certain emergency management/incident response personnel • Only the Incident Command System or an organization chart • A static system

B. CONCEPTS AND PRINCIPLES

NIMS is based on the premise that utilization of a common incident management framework will give emergency management/response personnel a flexible but standardized system for emergency management and incident response activities. NIMS is flexible because the system components can be utilized to develop plans, processes, procedures, agreements, and roles for all types of incidents; it is applicable to any incident regardless of cause, size, location, or complexity. Additionally, NIMS provides an organized set of standardized operational structures, which is critical in allowing disparate organizations and agencies to work together in a predictable, coordinated manner.

1. FLEXIBILITY

The components of NIMS are adaptable to any situation, from routine, local incidents to incidents requiring the activation of interstate mutual aid to those requiring a coordinated Federal response, whether planned (e.g., major sporting or community events), notice (e.g., hurricane) or no-notice (e.g., earthquake). This flexibility is essential for NIMS to be applicable across the full spectrum of potential incidents, including those that require multiagency, multijurisdictional (such as incidents that occur along international borders), and/or multidisciplinary coordination. Flexibility in the NIMS framework facilitates scalability of emergency management and incident response activities. NIMS also provides the flexibility for unique implementation in specified areas around the Nation. The National Integration Center (NIC), as appropriate, will review and support implementation plans, which reflect these individual requirements and organizational structures, for consistency with NIMS concepts and principles.

2. STANDARDIZATION

Flexibility to manage incidents of any size requires coordination and standardization among emergency management/response personnel and their affiliated organizations. NIMS provides a set of standardized organizational structures that improve integration and connectivity among jurisdictions and disciplines, starting with a common foundation of preparedness and planning. Personnel and organizations that have adopted the common NIMS framework are able to work together, thereby fostering cohesion among the various organizations involved in all aspects of an incident. NIMS also provides and promotes common terminology, which fosters more effective communication among agencies and organizations responding together to an incident.

C. OVERVIEW OF NIMS COMPONENTS

NIMS integrates existing best practices into a consistent, nationwide, systematic approach to incident management that is applicable at all levels of government, nongovernmental organizations (NGOs), and the private sector, and across functional disciplines in an all-hazards context. Five major components make up this systems approach: Preparedness, Communications and Information Management, Resource Management, Command and Management, and Ongoing Management and Maintenance.

1. NIMS COMPONENTS

The components of NIMS were not designed to stand alone, but to work together in a flexible, systematic manner to provide the national framework for incident management. A more detailed discussion of each component is included in subsequent sections of this document.

a. Preparedness

Effective emergency management and incident response activities begin with a host of preparedness activities conducted on an ongoing basis, in advance of any potential incident. Preparedness involves an integrated combination of assessment; planning; procedures and protocols; training and exercises; personnel qualifications, licensure, and certification; equipment certification; and evaluation and revision.

b. Communications and Information Management

Emergency management and incident response activities rely on communications and information systems that provide a common operating picture to all command and coordination sites. NIMS describes the requirements necessary for a standardized framework for communications and emphasizes the need for a common operating picture. This component is based on the concepts of interoperability, reliability, scalability, and portability, as well as the resiliency and redundancy of communications and information systems.

c. Resource Management

Resources (such as personnel, equipment, or supplies) are needed to support critical incident objectives. The flow of resources must be fluid and adaptable to the requirements of the incident. NIMS defines standardized mechanisms and establishes the resource management process to identify requirements, order and acquire, mobilize, track and report, recover and demobilize, reimburse, and inventory resources.

d. Command and Management

The Command and Management component of NIMS is designed to enable effective and efficient incident management and coordination by providing a flexible, standardized incident management structure. The structure is based on three key organizational constructs: the Incident Command System, Multiagency Coordination Systems, and Public Information.

e. Ongoing Management and Maintenance

Within the auspices of Ongoing Management and Maintenance, there are two components: the NIC and Supporting Technologies.

(1) National Integration Center

Homeland Security Presidential Directive 5 required the Secretary of Homeland Security to establish a mechanism for ensuring the ongoing management and maintenance of NIMS, including regular consultation with other Federal departments and agencies; State, tribal, and local stakeholders; and NGOs and the private sector. The NIC provides strategic direction, oversight, and coordination of NIMS and supports both routine maintenance and the continuous refinement of NIMS and its components. The NIC oversees the program and coordinates with Federal, State, tribal, and local partners in the development of compliance criteria and implementation activities. It provides guidance and support to jurisdictions and emergency management/response personnel and their affiliated organizations as they adopt or, consistent with their status, are encouraged to adopt the system. The NIC also oversees and coordinates the publication of NIMS and its related products. This oversight includes the review and certification of training courses and exercise information.

(2) Supporting Technologies

As NIMS and its related emergency management and incident response systems evolve, emergency management/response personnel will increasingly rely on technology and systems to implement and continuously refine NIMS. The NIC, in partnership with the Department of Homeland Security Science and Technology Directorate, oversees and coordinates the ongoing development of incident management-related technology, including strategic research and development.

COMPONENT I: PREPAREDNESS

NIMS provides the mechanisms for emergency management/response personnel[3] and their affiliated organizations to work collectively by offering the tools to enhance preparedness. Preparedness is achieved and maintained through a continuous cycle of planning, organizing, training, equipping, exercising, evaluating, and taking corrective action. Ongoing preparedness efforts among all those involved in emergency management and incident response activities ensure coordination during times of crisis. Moreover, preparedness facilitates efficient and effective emergency management and incident response activities.

This component describes specific measures and capabilities that emergency management/response personnel and their affiliated organizations should develop and incorporate into their overall preparedness programs to enhance the operational preparedness necessary for all-hazards emergency management and incident response activities. In developing, refining, and expanding preparedness programs and activities within their jurisdictions and/or organizations, emergency management/response personnel should leverage existing preparedness efforts and collaborative relationships to the greatest extent possible. Personal preparedness, while an important element of homeland security, is distinct from the operational preparedness of our Nation's emergency management and incident response capabilities and is beyond the scope of NIMS.

A. CONCEPTS AND PRINCIPLES

Within NIMS, preparedness focuses on the following elements: planning; procedures and protocols; training and exercises; personnel qualifications, licensure, and certification; and equipment certification. Effective adoption, implementation, and training of all NIMS components in advance of an incident or planned event will facilitate collaborative emergency management and incident response activities. Preparedness is a foundational step in emergency management and incident response; therefore, the concepts and principles that form the basis for preparedness are an integration of the concepts and principles of all NIMS components.

1. UNIFIED APPROACH

Preparedness requires a unified approach to emergency management and incident response activities. To achieve this, components of NIMS should be integrated within a jurisdiction's or organization's emergency management and incident response structure. Specifically, preparedness should be integrated into communications and information management, resource management, and command and management to form an effective system. Additionally, the unified-approach concept is at the core of the Command and Management component, as it is based on chain of command, unity of command, unity of effort, and when implemented, Unified Command. These characteristics allow organizations with

---

[3] Emergency management/response personnel include Federal, State, territorial, tribal, substate regional, and local governments, nongovernmental organizations, private-sector organizations, critical infrastructure owners and operators, and all other organizations and individuals who assume an emergency management role.

different jurisdictional, geographical, or functional responsibilities, authorities, and resources to coordinate, plan, and interact effectively in support of a commonly recognized objective.

2. LEVELS OF CAPABILITY

Preparedness involves actions to establish and sustain necessary capabilities to execute a full range of emergency management and incident response activities. For NIMS to function effectively, jurisdictions and organizations should set expectations about the capabilities and resources that will be provided before, during, and after an incident. The inventorying and categorizing of resources available for an incident or planned event is a critical element of preparedness, as it helps to establish and verify the level of capability needed. Additionally, the concept of identifying this level of capability is woven throughout the components of NIMS, including the credentialing system.

B. ACHIEVING PREPAREDNESS

Individual jurisdictions should prepare in advance of an incident, in coordination with and supported by Federal and State partners, nongovernmental organizations (NGOs), and the private sector, as appropriate. In order for successful emergency management and incident response to occur, emergency management/response personnel and their affiliated organizations must have a clear understanding of their roles and responsibilities. This clarity is essential not only for emergency management/response personnel, but also for those acting in a policy, coordination, or support role.

- *Policy Role:* Development, revision, signing, and/or formalization of policies, procedures, mutual aid agreements, and assistance agreements and/or plans relating to emergency management and incident response programs and activities.
- *Coordination Role:* Resource management or any other necessary coordination efforts required for emergency management and incident response programs and activities.
- *Support Role:* Provision of assistance for emergency management and incident response programs and activities.

1. RELATIONSHIP BETWEEN NIMS AND OTHER PREPAREDNESS EFFORTS

To achieve national preparedness and coordinated response, emergency management and incident response activities should be coordinated at all levels of government and should include NGOs and the private sector, where appropriate. Homeland Security Presidential Directive 5 (HSPD–5) established a single, comprehensive approach to incident management, with the objective of ensuring that all levels of government across the Nation have the capability to work together efficiently and effectively. Several other Homeland Security Presidential Directives are inextricably linked with HSPD–5, as they deal directly with national preparedness and the protection of critical infrastructure. These directives are discussed more fully below.

a. Homeland Security Presidential Directive 7, "Critical Infrastructure Identification, Prioritization, and Protection"

HSPD–7 directed the Department of Homeland Security (DHS) to establish a national policy for Federal departments and agencies to identify and prioritize critical infrastructure and key resources (CIKR) in order to prevent, deter, and mitigate the effects of deliberate efforts to destroy, incapacitate, or exploit them. Federal departments and agencies are to work with State, tribal, and local governments, NGOs, and the private sector to accomplish this objective. This effort includes the development, implementation, and ongoing management and maintenance of the *National Infrastructure Protection Plan* (NIPP). The NIPP and its complementary Sector-Specific Plans provide the unifying structure for integrating existing and future CIKR protection activities.

b. Homeland Security Presidential Directive 8, "National Preparedness"

HSPD–8 directed DHS to lead a national initiative to develop a National Preparedness System—a common, unified approach to "strengthen the preparedness of the United States to prevent and respond to threatened or actual domestic terrorist attacks, major disasters, and other emergencies." The requirements of HSPD–8 led to the National Preparedness Guidelines, which were developed to provide the means for the Nation to answer three fundamental questions:

- How prepared do we need to be?
- How prepared are we?
- How do we prioritize efforts to close the gap?

HSPD–8 also required DHS to develop mechanisms for the improved delivery of Federal preparedness assistance to State, tribal, and local governments and to strengthen the Nation's preparedness capabilities. Annex I to HSPD-8, titled "National Planning," establishes a comprehensive approach to national planning and provides guidance for conducting planning in accordance with the *National Strategy for Homeland Security*. Annex I calls for the development and updating of an Integrated Planning System (IPS). Fifteen National Planning Scenarios were developed to illustrate the range, scope, magnitude, and complexity of incidents for which the Nation should prepare. Using this wide range of possible scenarios, including terrorism, natural disasters, and health emergencies, helps reduce uncertainty in planning.

After identifying the most important performance needs across the scenarios, DHS then developed the Target Capabilities List (TCL), designed to guide efforts to build a national network of capabilities that will be available when and where they are needed. The TCL outlines an all-hazards approach to development of capabilities that will be needed for natural or manmade disasters or other major incidents, and defines the primary roles that all levels of government, NGOs, the private sector, and individuals have in national preparedness. The capabilities provide the means to accomplish a mission and achieve desired outcomes by performing critical tasks, under specified conditions, to target levels of performance. Capabilities are delivered by appropriate combinations of properly planned, organized, equipped, trained, and exercised personnel.

2. NIMS AND ITS RELATIONSHIP TO THE NATIONAL RESPONSE FRAMEWORK

NIMS provides the template for the management of incidents, regardless of cause, size, location, or complexity. This template establishes the structure, concepts, principles, processes, and language for the effective employment of capabilities nationally, whether those capabilities reside with Federal, State, tribal, or local jurisdictions or with the private sector or NGOs.

The *National Response Framework* (NRF), which superseded the National Response Plan, is an all-hazards framework that builds upon NIMS and describes additional specific Federal roles and structures for incidents in which Federal resources are involved.

> **The NRF is a guide to how the Nation conducts all-hazards response.**

The NRF provides the structure and mechanisms for national-level policy and operational direction for incident management to ensure timely and effective Federal support to State, tribal, and local related activities. The NRF is applicable to all Federal departments and agencies that participate in operations requiring a coordinated Federal response.

NIMS and the NRF are designed to improve the Nation's incident management capabilities and overall efficiency. During incidents requiring coordinated Federal support, the NRF provides the guidelines and procedures to integrate capabilities and resources into a cohesive, coordinated, and seamless national framework for incident management.

> **NIMS and the NRF are designed to ensure that local jurisdictions retain command, control, and authority over response activities for their jurisdictional areas.**

A basic premise of both NIMS and the NRF is that incidents typically be managed at the local level first. In the vast majority of incidents, local resources and local mutual aid agreements and assistance agreements will provide the first line of emergency management and incident response. If additional or specialized resources or capabilities are needed, Governors may request Federal assistance; however, NIMS is based on the concept that local jurisdictions retain command, control, and authority over response activities for their jurisdictional areas. Adhering to NIMS allows local agencies to better utilize incoming resources.

The fundamental role of preparedness in emergency management and incident response is a universal concept incorporated in both NIMS and the NRF. Though the specific elements of preparedness described within each document may vary slightly, the concepts remain complementary. The key elements found within the Preparedness component of NIMS and the NRF are described and organized in a fashion to best assist stakeholders in the development of efficient, effective emergency management and incident response capabilities.

3. PREPAREDNESS ROLES

Preparedness activities should be coordinated among all appropriate agencies and organizations within the jurisdiction, as well as across jurisdictions. NGOs and the private sector should be involved in these efforts, as they often provide incident-related services, and are the owners and operators of critical infrastructure and key resources that may be involved in emergency management and incident response. Though not integrated directly into NIMS, individuals play a critical role in preparedness and are expected to prepare themselves and their families for all types of potential incidents. Jurisdictions should have outreach programs to promote and support individual and community preparedness (e.g., public education, training sessions, demonstrations), including preparedness of those with special needs.

a. Preparedness Organizations

Preparedness organizations provide coordination for emergency management and incident response activities before an incident or planned event. These organizations range from groups of individuals to small committees to large standing organizations that represent a wide variety of committees, planning groups, or other organizations (e.g., Citizen Corps, Community Emergency Response Teams, Local Emergency Planning Committees, Critical Infrastructure Sector Coordinating Councils). Preparedness organizations should meet regularly and coordinate with one another to ensure an appropriate focus on helping jurisdictions and groups of jurisdictions to meet their preparedness needs.

The needs of the jurisdictions involved will dictate how frequently such organizations should conduct their business, as well as how they are structured. When preparedness activities routinely need to be accomplished across jurisdictions, preparedness organizations should be multijurisdictional and/or multiagency and include critical infrastructure owners and operators, NGOs, and the private sector, when relevant. Memorandums or agreements should be established between necessary parties so that each will be aware of the capabilities, expectations, and roles of the others.

Preparedness organizations may take the following actions, among others:

- Establish and coordinate emergency operations plans, protocols, and procedures, including public communications and awareness.
- Integrate and coordinate the activities and functions within their purview.
- Establish the standards, guidelines, and protocols necessary to promote interoperability and consideration for responder safety.
- Adopt standards, guidelines, and procedures for requesting and providing resources.
- Identify resources and other requirements and set priorities for their use.
- Encourage training, exercises, evaluation, and corrective action programs.
- Ensure the establishment and maintenance of necessary mutual aid agreements and assistance agreements and outreach to NGOs and the private sector.
- Use Multiagency Coordination Systems, as needed and where appropriate, for planned events (such as parades or sporting events) or for specific types of incidents (such as pandemic influenza or hurricanes).[4]
- Plan for operational scientific support, which can be done at each level of government, and contribute ideas to ongoing research and development of new technologies.[5]
- Conduct after-action reviews to strengthen future preparedness.

b. Elected and Appointed Officials

Elected and appointed officials should have a clear understanding of their roles and responsibilities for successful emergency management and incident response. These officials include administrative and political personnel, as well as department/agency administrators who have leadership roles in a jurisdiction, including legislators and chief executives, whether elected (e.g., Governors, mayors, sheriffs, tribal leaders, and county executives) or appointed (e.g., county administrators and city managers). Although their roles may require providing direction and guidance to constituents during an incident, their

---

[4] See page 64, Component IV: Command and Management, Multiagency Coordination Systems.
[5] See page 79, Component V: Ongoing Management and Maintenance, Supporting Technologies.

day-to-day activities do not necessarily focus on emergency management and incident response.

To better serve their constituents, elected and appointed officials should do the following:

- Understand, commit to, and receive training on NIMS and participate in exercises.
- Maintain an understanding of basic emergency management, continuity of operations and continuity of government plans, jurisdictional response capabilities, and initiation of disaster declarations.
- Lead and encourage preparedness efforts within the community, agencies of the jurisdiction, NGOs, and the private sector, as appropriate.
- Help to establish relationships (including mutual aid agreements and assistance agreements) with other jurisdictions and, as appropriate, NGOs and the private sector.
- Support and encourage participation in mitigation efforts within the jurisdiction and, as appropriate, with NGOs and the private sector.
- Provide guidance to their jurisdictions, departments, and/or agencies, with clearly stated policies for NIMS implementation.
- Understand laws and regulations in their jurisdictions that pertain to emergency management and incident response.
- Maintain awareness of CIKR within their jurisdictions, potential incident impacts, and restoration priorities.

Elected and appointed officials may also be called upon to help shape and revise laws, policies, and budgets to aid in preparedness efforts and to improve emergency management and incident response activities.

An incident may have a mix of political, economic, social, environmental, public safety, public health, and financial implications with potentially serious long-term effects. Frequently, incidents require a coordinated response (across agencies, jurisdictions, and/or including NGOs and the private sector), during which elected and appointed officials must make difficult decisions under crisis conditions. Elected and appointed officials should be aware of how NIMS can work to ensure cooperative response efforts, thereby minimizing the potential implications of an incident.

(1) Elected and Appointed Officials During an Incident

Generally, elected and appointed officials are not at the scene of the incident, but should have the ability to communicate and meet with the Incident Commander (IC)/Unified Command (UC), as necessary. Depending on the nature of the incident or level of the overall emergency, elected and appointed officials could function from the following locations:

- The agency or jurisdictional offices.
- An Emergency Operations Center.
- A location housing multiagency coordination.

> **Major Responsibilities of Elected and Appointed Officials**
>
> - Clearly state agency/jurisdiction policy
> - Evaluate effectiveness and correct deficiencies
> - Support a multiagency approach

Elected and appointed officials should provide input on policy, direction, and authority to the IC/UC. Proper coordination between elected and appointed officials and the IC/UC can be crucial to the successful management of an incident. Elected and appointed officials should clearly communicate views to the IC/UC. As time and agency policy dictate, the following considerations should be clearly communicated, documented, and provided to the IC/UC:

- Safety considerations.
- Environmental issues.
- Legal and policy limitations.
- Issues relating to critical infrastructure services or restoration.
- Economic, political, and social concerns.
- Cost considerations.

In some circumstances, if information is not delineated in policies or laws, it should be defined through a formal delegation of authority or letter of expectation.

c. Nongovernmental Organizations

NGOs, such as community-based, faith-based, or national organizations (e.g., the Salvation Army, National Voluntary Organizations Active in Disaster, American Red Cross), play vital roles in emergency management and incident response activities. NGOs that have the capacity and desire to be involved should be fully integrated into a jurisdiction's preparedness efforts, especially in planning, training, and exercises. Furthermore, memorandums of agreement should be established with NGOs prior to an incident so that each organization is aware of the capabilities, expectations, and roles of others.

It is recommended that key executives and administrators of NGOs use NIMS for planned events or incidents, because its use improves the organizations' ability to integrate into incident management. While compliance with NIMS is not mandated for NGOs, adhering to NIMS procedures and terminology, and requiring staff with disaster-related missions to take appropriate training, will support the continued integration of the NGOs into a jurisdiction's preparedness efforts.

d. Private Sector

The private sector plays a vital role in emergency management and incident response and should be incorporated into all aspects of NIMS. Utilities, industries, corporations, businesses, and professional and trade associations typically are involved in critical aspects of emergency response and incident management. These organizations should prepare for all-hazards incidents that may affect their ability to deliver goods and services. It is essential that private-sector organizations directly involved in emergency management and incident response, or identified as a component of critical infrastructure (e.g., hospitals, public and private utility companies, schools), be included, as appropriate, in a jurisdiction's preparedness efforts. Although private-sector entities cannot be required to be NIMS compliant, it is strongly encouraged that those private-sector organizations that are directly involved in response operations have their response personnel receive NIMS training and that the response elements of their organization be NIMS compliant.

Governments at all levels should work with the private sector to establish a common set of expectations consistent with Federal, State, tribal, and local roles, responsibilities, and methods of operations. These expectations should be widely disseminated and the necessary training and practical exercises conducted so that they are thoroughly understood in advance of an actual incident. These expectations are particularly important with respect to private-sector organizations involved in CIKR areas. In addition, private-sector organizations may wish to consider entering into assistance agreements with governments or other private-sector organizations to clarify the respective capabilities, roles, and expectations of the parties involved in preparing for and responding to an incident. Finally, the private sector may be a source for best practices in emergency management and incident response.

Academia also plays a significant role in NIMS. Many academic institutions assist in providing NIMS training to responders and community leaders. Additionally, many courses of study include NIMS training and concepts in their curricula. The academic community is also a primary vehicle for the development of new concepts and principles.

4. PREPAREDNESS ELEMENTS

Preparedness efforts should validate and maintain plans, policies, and procedures, describing how they will prioritize, coordinate, manage, and support information and resources. The elements described below build the foundation necessary for efficient and effective response and recovery. Ongoing support is provided by the National Integration Center (NIC) in the following areas: training and exercises; personnel qualifications, licensure, and certification; and equipment certification.[6]

a. Preparedness Planning

Plans should be realistic, scalable, and applicable to all types of incidents, from daily occurrences to incidents requiring the activation of interstate mutual aid to those requiring a coordinated Federal response. Plans should form the basis of training and be exercised periodically to ensure that all individuals involved in response are able to execute their assigned tasks. It is essential that plans address training and exercising and allow for the incorporation of after-action reviews, lessons learned, and corrective actions, with responsibility agreements following any major incident or exercise. Plans should be updated periodically to reflect changes in the emergency management and incident response environment, as well as any institutional or organizational changes.

Plans should describe how personnel, equipment, and other governmental and nongovernmental resources will be used to support emergency management and incident response requirements. Plans are the operational core of preparedness and provide mechanisms for setting priorities, integrating multiple jurisdictions/organizations and functions, establishing collaborative relationships, and ensuring that communications and other systems effectively support the full spectrum of emergency management and incident response activities. Plans should also incorporate strategies for maintaining continuity of government and continuity of operations during and after incidents, provide mechanisms to ensure resiliency of critical infrastructure and economic stability of communities, and incorporate the advance planning associated with responder protection, resource management, and communications and information management.

Plans should integrate all relevant departments, agencies, and organizations (including NGOs and the private sector, where appropriate) to facilitate coordinated emergency management and incident response activities. Where appropriate, plans should incorporate a clearly defined process for seeking and requesting assistance from necessary departments, agencies, or organizations. While it is recognized that jurisdictions and organizations will develop multiple types of plans, such as response, mitigation, and recovery plans, it is essential that these plans be coordinated and complement one another. State, tribal, and local governments are encouraged to comply with the Integrated Planning

---

[6] See page 75, Component V: Ongoing Management and Maintenance, National Integration Center.

System (IPS) by using Comprehensive Preparedness Guide (CPG) 101, "Producing Operations Plans for State, Territorial, Tribal, and Local Governments." CPG 101 meets the Annex I requirement that IPS include a "guide for all-hazards planning . . . that can be used at Federal, State, local, and tribal levels to assist the planning process." IPS is flexible enough to accommodate the many planning formats, styles, and processes used by State, tribal, and local governments. Over time, the use of IPS is expected to facilitate standardization of plans across the United States at all levels of government and enhance preparedness. Together IPS and CPG 101 support national vertical integration by clearly articulating Federal planning procedures to State, tribal, and local governments and by establishing a consistent planning process across all levels of government.

Each jurisdiction, in coordination with appropriate agencies and organizations, should develop plans that define the scope of necessary activities for preparedness, emergency management, and incident response for that jurisdiction. As appropriate, jurisdictions should also develop scenario-specific plans or annexes derived from their threat assessment. These plans should describe organizational structures, roles and responsibilities, policies, and protocols for providing support; should be flexible enough for use in all incidents; and should be comprehensive enough to meet the wide variety of public needs that may arise. While preparedness of the public is generally beyond the scope of NIMS, plans should also include public awareness, education, and communications plans and protocols.

(1) Continuity Capability

Recent natural and manmade disasters have demonstrated the need for a robust continuity capability at the Federal, State, territorial, tribal, and local levels, as well as within the private sector, in order to ensure the preservation of our form of government under the Constitution and the continuation of essential functions under all conditions. Ensuring that the right leadership, support staff, communications, facilities, infrastructure, and other resources with the right continuity planning and program management are available to support a jurisdiction is critical to the success of emergency management and incident response operations.

The goal of a robust continuity capability is to have the resiliency to confront any challenge, threat, or vulnerability. Continuity planning should be instituted within all organizations—to include all levels of government and the private sector—and especially within those organizations that support the National Essential Functions found in National Security Presidential Directive 51/Homeland Security Presidential Directive 20 (NSPD-51/HSPD-20), "National Continuity Policy," dated May 4, 2007. NSPD-51/HSPD-20 and Federal Continuity Directive 1, dated February 4, 2007, outline the continuity requirements for all Federal departments and agencies (with guidance for non-Federal organizations). These requirements include such things as essential functions, orders of succession, delegations of authority, continuity facilities, continuity communications, vital records management, and human capital.

(2) Mutual Aid Agreements and Assistance Agreements

Mutual aid agreements and assistance agreements are agreements between agencies, organizations, and jurisdictions that provide a mechanism to quickly obtain emergency assistance in the form of personnel, equipment, materials, and other associated services. The primary objective is to facilitate rapid, short-term deployment of emergency support prior to, during, and after an incident. A signed agreement does not obligate the provision or receipt of aid, but rather provides a tool for use should the incident dictate a need. There are several types of these kinds of agreements, including but not limited to the following:

> Agreements, preferably written, should include the following elements or provisions:
> - **Definitions of key terms used in the agreement**
> - **Roles and responsibilities of individual parties**
> - **Procedures for requesting and providing assistance**
> - **Procedures, authorities, and rules for payment, reimbursement, and allocation of costs**
> - **Notification procedures**
> - **Protocols for interoperable communications**
> - **Relationships with other agreements among jurisdictions**
> - **Workers' compensation**
> - **Treatment of liability and immunity**
> - **Recognition of qualifications, licensure, and certifications**
> - **Sharing agreements, as required**
> - **Termination clause**

- *Automatic Mutual Aid:* Agreements that permit the automatic dispatch and response of requested resources without incident-specific approvals. These agreements are usually basic contracts; some may be informal accords.
- *Local Mutual Aid:* Agreements between neighboring jurisdictions or organizations that involve a formal request for assistance and generally cover a larger geographic area than automatic mutual aid.
- *Regional Mutual Aid:* Substate regional mutual aid agreements between multiple jurisdictions that are often sponsored by a council of governments or a similar regional body.
- *Statewide/Intrastate Mutual Aid:* Agreements, often coordinated through the State, that incorporate both State and local governmental and nongovernmental resources in an attempt to increase preparedness statewide.
- *Interstate Agreements:* Out-of-State assistance through the Emergency Management Assistance Compact (EMAC) or other formal State-to-State agreements that support the response effort.
- *International Agreements:* Agreements between the United States and other nations for the exchange of Federal assets in an emergency.
- *Other Agreements:* Any agreement, whether formal or informal, used to request or provide assistance and/or resources among jurisdictions at any level of government (including foreign), NGOs, or the private sector.

Jurisdictions should be party to agreements with the appropriate jurisdictions and/or organizations (including NGOs and the private sector, where appropriate) from which they expect to receive, or to which they expect to provide, assistance. States should participate in interstate compacts and look to establish intrastate agreements that encompass all local jurisdictions. Authorized officials from each of the participating jurisdictions and/or organizations should collectively approve all mutual aid agreements and assistance agreements.

Memorandums of understanding and memorandums of agreement are needed with the private sector and NGOs, including community-based, faith-based, and national organizations such as the American Red Cross and the Salvation Army, to facilitate the timely delivery of assistance during incidents.

b. Procedures and Protocols

Procedures and protocols should detail the specific actions to implement a plan or system. All emergency management/response personnel and their affiliated organizations should develop procedures and protocols that translate into specific, action-oriented checklists for use during incident response operations.

Procedures are documented and implemented with checklists; resource listings; maps, charts, and other pertinent data; mechanisms for notifying staff; processes for obtaining and using equipment, supplies, and vehicles; methods of obtaining mutual aid agreements and assistance agreements; mechanisms for reporting information to Department Operations Centers and Emergency Operations Centers; and communications operating instructions, including connectivity among governments, NGOs, and the private sector.

There are four standard levels of procedural documents:

- ***Standard Operating Procedure or Operations Manual:*** Complete reference document that provides the purpose, authorities, duration, and details for the preferred method of performing a single function or a number of interrelated functions in a uniform manner.
- ***Field Operations Guide or Incident Management Handbook:*** Durable pocket or desk guide that contains essential information required to perform specific assignments or functions.
- ***Mobilization Guide:*** Reference document used by agencies/organizations outlining agreements, processes, and procedures used by all participating organizations for activating, assembling, and transporting resources.
- ***Job Aid:*** Checklist or other visual aid intended to ensure that specific steps for completing a task or assignment are accomplished. Job aids serve as training aids to teach individuals how to complete specific job tasks.

Protocols are sets of established guidelines for actions (which may be designated by individuals, teams, functions, or capabilities) under various specified conditions. Establishing protocols provides for the standing orders, authorizations, and delegations necessary to permit the rapid execution of a task, function, or a number of interrelated functions without having to seek permission. Protocols permit specific personnel—based on training and delegation of authority—to assess a situation, take immediate steps to intervene, and escalate their efforts to a specific level before further guidance or authorizations are required.

c. Training and Exercises

Personnel with roles in emergency management and incident response at all levels of government—including persons with leadership positions, such as elected and appointed officials—should be appropriately trained to improve all-hazards capabilities nationwide. Additionally, NGOs and private-sector entities with direct roles in response operations should be strongly encouraged to participate in NIMS training and exercises. Standardized NIMS training courses focused on the structure and operational coordination processes and systems, together with courses focused on discipline-specific and agency-specific expertise, help to ensure that emergency management/response personnel can function together effectively during an incident. Training and exercises should be specifically tailored to the responsibilities of the personnel involved in incident management. Mentoring or shadowing opportunities, to allow less experienced personnel to observe those with more experience during an actual incident, should be incorporated to enhance training and exercising. Additionally, exercises should be designed to allow personnel to simulate multiple command, supervisory, or leadership roles whenever possible.

NIMS training levels are dependent on the individual's, jurisdiction's, or organization's level of involvement in emergency management and incident response activities.

Training should allow practitioners to:

- Use the concepts and principles of NIMS in exercises, planned events, and actual incidents.
- Become more comfortable using NIMS, including the Incident Command System.

To improve NIMS performance, emergency management/response personnel should also participate in realistic exercises—including multidisciplinary, multijurisdictional incidents, and NGO and private-sector interaction—to improve coordination and interoperability. Thorough exercising of NIMS components may be done using a single exercise or a series of exercises, each of which evaluates specific aspects of NIMS and its components.

> Exercises should contain a mechanism for incorporating corrective actions into the planning process.

Exercises should be conducted with parties identified in strategic and operational plans (e.g., the emergency operations plan), including departments, agencies, partners in mutual aid agreements and assistance agreements, NGOs, and the private sector. Exercises should contain a mechanism for incorporating corrective actions and lessons learned from incidents into the planning process. For guidance on exercise design, methodology, and evaluation, refer to the Homeland Security Exercise and Evaluation Program or other exercise development tools. Exercises should also cover the following:

- All aspects of a plan, particularly the processes and procedures for activating local, intrastate, and/or interstate mutual aid agreements and assistance agreements.
- Knowledge needed to activate those agreements.

d. Personnel Qualifications and Certification

A critical element of NIMS preparedness is the use of national standards that allow for common or compatible structures for the qualification, licensure, and certification of emergency management/response personnel.[7] Standards will help ensure that these personnel possess the minimum knowledge, skills, and experience necessary to execute incident management and emergency response activities safely and effectively. Standards typically include training, experience, credentialing, validation, and physical and medical fitness. Federal, State, tribal, and local certifying agencies, and professional and private organizations with personnel involved in emergency management and incident response, are encouraged to credential those individuals in their respective disciplines or jurisdictions.

---

[7] See page 40, Component III: Resource Management, Credentialing.

The baseline criteria for this voluntary credentialing will be established by the NIC after consultation with appropriate experts, partners, and/or recognized authoritative bodies, which will detail the standards associated with the minimum thresholds for specific emergency management positions, allowing those credentialed personnel to participate, as needed, in national-level incidents.

e. Equipment Certification

Emergency management/response personnel and their affiliated organizations rely on various types and kinds of equipment to perform essential tasks.[8] A critical component of preparedness is the acquisition of equipment that will perform to certain standards (as designated by organizations such as the National Fire Protection Association or National Institute of Standards and Technology), including the capability to be interoperable with equipment used by other jurisdictions or participating organizations.[9] Associated with this is the need to have a common understanding of the abilities of distinct types of equipment, to allow for better planning before an incident and rapid scaling and flexibility in meeting the needs of an incident.

5. MITIGATION

Mitigation is an important element of emergency management and incident response. It provides a critical foundation in the effort to reduce the loss of life and property and to minimize damage to the environment from natural or manmade disasters by avoiding or lessening the impact of a disaster. Mitigation provides value to the public by creating safer communities and impeding the cycle of disaster damage, reconstruction, and repeated damage. Mitigative actions should effectively be coordinated between the IC/UC and the operator of the CIKR facilities. These activities or actions, in most cases, will have a long-term sustained effect. Risk management—the process for measuring or assessing risk and developing strategies to manage it—is an essential aspect of mitigation. Risk management strategies may include avoiding the risk (e.g., removing structures in floodplains), reducing the negative effect of the risk (e.g., hardening buildings by placing barriers around them), or accepting some or all of the consequences of a particular risk.

Examples of mitigation activities include the following:

- Ongoing public education and outreach activities designed to reduce loss of life and destruction of property.
- Complying with or exceeding floodplain management and land-use regulations.
- Enforcing stringent building codes, seismic design standards, and wind-bracing requirements for new construction, or repairing or retrofitting existing buildings.
- Supporting measures to ensure the protection and resilience of CIKR designed to ensure business continuity and the economic stability of communities.
- Acquiring damaged homes or businesses in flood-prone areas, relocating the structures, and returning the property to open space, wetlands, or recreational uses.
- Identifying, utilizing, and refurbishing shelters and safe rooms to help protect people in their homes, public buildings, and schools in hurricane- and tornado-prone areas.
- Implementing a vital records program at all levels of government to prevent loss of crucial documents and records.

---

[8] See page 31, Component III: Resource Management for more information on equipment certification.
[9] See page 75, Component V: Ongoing Management and Maintenance, National Integration Center.

- Intelligence sharing and linkage leading to other law enforcement activities, such as infiltration of a terrorist cell to prevent an attack.
- Periodic remapping of hazard or potential hazard zones, using geospatial techniques.
- Management of data regarding historical incidents to support strategic planning and analysis.
- Development of hazard-specific evacuation routes.

COMPONENT II:
COMMUNICATIONS AND
INFORMATION MANAGEMENT

Effective emergency management and incident response activities rely on flexible communications and information systems that provide a common operating picture to emergency management/response personnel[10] and their affiliated organizations. Establishing and maintaining a common operating picture and ensuring accessibility and interoperability are the principal goals of the Communications and Information Management component of NIMS. Properly planned, established, and applied communications enable the dissemination of information among command and support elements and, as appropriate, cooperating agencies and organizations.

Incident communications are facilitated through the development and use of common communications plans and interoperable communications equipment, processes, standards, and architectures. During an incident, this integrated approach links the operational and support units of the various organizations to maintain communications connectivity and situational awareness. Communications and information management planning should address the incident-related policies, equipment, systems, standards, and training necessary to achieve integrated communications.

A. CONCEPTS AND PRINCIPLES

The underlying concepts and principles of this component reinforce the use of a flexible communications and information system in which emergency management/response personnel can maintain a constant flow of information during an incident. These concepts and principles emphasize the need for and maintenance of a common operating picture; interoperability; reliability, scalability, and portability; and resiliency and redundancy of any system and its components.

1. COMMON OPERATING PICTURE

A common operating picture is established and maintained by gathering, collating, synthesizing, and disseminating incident information to all appropriate parties. Achieving a common operating picture allows on-scene and off-scene personnel—such as those at the Incident Command Post, Emergency Operations Center (EOC), or within a Multiagency Coordination Group—to have the same information about the incident, including the availability and location of resources and the status of assistance requests. Additionally, a common operating picture offers an incident overview that enables the Incident Commander (IC),

> **Common Operating Picture**
>
> **An overview of an incident created by collating and gathering information—such as traffic, weather, actual damage, resource availability—of any type (voice, data, etc.) from agencies/organizations in order to support decisionmaking**

---

[10] Emergency management/response personnel include Federal, State, territorial, tribal, substate regional, and local governments, nongovernmental organizations, private-sector organizations, critical infrastructure owners and operators, and all other organizations and individuals who assume an emergency management role.

Unified Command (UC), and supporting agencies and organizations to make effective, consistent, and timely decisions. In order to maintain situational awareness, communications and incident information must be updated continually. Having a common operating picture during an incident helps to ensure consistency for all emergency management/response personnel engaged in an incident.

2. INTEROPERABILITY

Communications interoperability allows emergency management/response personnel and their affiliated organizations to communicate within and across agencies and jurisdictions via voice, data, or video in real time, when needed, and when authorized. It is essential that these communications systems be capable of interoperability, as successful emergency management and incident response operations require the continuous flow of critical information among jurisdictions, disciplines, organizations, and agencies.

Interoperability planning requires accounting for emergency management and incident response contingencies and challenges. Interoperability plans should include considerations of governance, standard operating procedures (SOPs), technology, training and exercises, and usage within the context of the stress and chaos of a major response effort. Coordinated decisionmaking between agencies and jurisdictions is necessary to establish proper and coherent governance and is critical to achieving interoperability. Agreements and SOPs should clearly articulate the processes, procedures, and protocols necessary to achieve interoperability.

3. RELIABILITY, SCALABILITY, AND PORTABILITY

Communications and information systems should be designed to be flexible, reliable, and scalable in order to function in any type of incident, regardless of cause, size, location, or complexity. They should be suitable for operations within a single jurisdiction or agency, a single jurisdiction with multiagency involvement, or multiple jurisdictions with multiagency involvement. Communications systems should be applicable and acceptable to users, readily adaptable to new technology, and reliable in the context of any incident to which emergency management/response personnel would be expected to respond.

Portability of radio technologies, protocols, and frequencies among emergency management/response personnel will allow for the successful and efficient integration, transport, and deployment of communications systems when necessary. Portability includes the standardized assignment of radio channels across jurisdictions, which allows responders to participate in an incident outside their jurisdiction and still use familiar equipment.

Scalability differs from portability in that scalability allows responders to increase the number of users on a system, while portability facilitates the interaction of systems that are normally distinct.

4. RESILIENCY AND REDUNDANCY

Resiliency is the ability of communications systems to withstand and continue to perform after damage or loss of infrastructure. It requires communications systems to avoid relying solely on a sophisticated but vulnerable network of support systems. Prudent resiliency practices could include hardened dispatch centers and transmission systems or infrastructure that can withstand known risks. Repeater antenna sites, for example, are equipped with independent power systems to ensure their continued functionality during a power failure.

Redundancy is another essential element of a jurisdiction's/organization's communications structure. Although the duplication of identical services is one method of achieving redundancy, it also derives from the ability to communicate through diverse, alternative methods when standard capabilities suffer damage. For example, a public safety agency might have a high-tech voice 400-megahertz system that is used as the primary dispatch system, but maintain a redundant VHF system in its vehicles that would be able to contact the dispatch center in the event that the primary system is rendered inoperable. Resiliency and redundancy are critical to ensuring communications flow during an incident.

B. MANAGEMENT CHARACTERISTICS

Emergency management/response personnel should be able to manage incident communications and information effectively. Regardless of the communications method or the information being transmitted, procedures and protocols should be followed. As technologies change and the methods of exchanging information improve, management procedures likewise should evolve.

1. STANDARDIZED COMMUNICATION TYPES

Successful communications and information management require that emergency management/response personnel and their affiliated organizations use standardized communications types. The determination of the individual or agency/organization responsible for these communications is discussed in the Command and Management component and in Appendix B. The following is a list of standardized communication types:[11]

- **Strategic Communications:** High-level directions, including resource priority decisions, roles and responsibilities determinations, and overall incident response courses of action.
- **Tactical Communications:** Communications between command and support elements and, as appropriate, cooperating agencies and organizations.
- **Support Communications:** Coordination in support of strategic and tactical communications (for example, communications among hospitals concerning resource ordering, dispatching, and tracking from logistics centers; traffic and public works communications).
- **Public Address Communications:** Emergency alerts and warnings, press conferences, etc.[12]

2. POLICY AND PLANNING

Coordinated communications policy and planning provides the basis for effective communications and information management. Although communications and information management is important during routine operations, well-established procedures and protocols become critical during incident response activities. Careful planning should

---

[11] See page 70, Component IV: Command and Management, Public Information, and page 103, Appendix B: Incident Command System, Planning Section Chief.
[12] See page 70, Component IV, Command and Management, Public Information.

determine what communications systems and platforms will be used, who can use them, what information is essential in different environments, the technical parameters of all equipment and systems, and other relevant considerations.

Information flow among all stakeholders is crucial, but interoperability presents additional challenges when nongovernmental organizations (NGOs), the private sector, and critical infrastructure owners and operators are considered. All relevant stakeholders should be involved in meetings and planning sessions in order to formulate more thorough and integrated communications plans and strategies. Technology and equipment standards also should be shared when appropriate, to provide stakeholders with the opportunity to be interoperable and compatible.

Sound communications management policies and plans should include information about the following aspects of communications and information management:

- Information needs should be defined by the jurisdiction/organization. These needs are often met at the Federal, State, tribal, and local levels, in concert with NGOs and the private sector, and primarily through preparedness organizations.

- The jurisdiction's or organization's information management system should provide guidance, standards, and tools to enable the integration of information needs into a common operating picture when needed.

- Procedures and protocols for the release of warnings, incident notifications, public communications, and other critical information are disseminated through a defined combination of networks used by EOCs. Notifications are made to the appropriate jurisdictional levels and to NGOs and the private sector through defined mechanisms specified in emergency operations plans and Incident Action Plans.

- Agencies at all levels should plan in advance for the effective and efficient use of information management technologies (e.g., computers, networks, and information-sharing mechanisms) to integrate all command, coordination, and support functions involved in incident management and to enable the sharing of critical information and the cataloging of required corrective actions.

3. AGREEMENTS

All parties identified in the planning process used in a jurisdiction's emergency operations plan need to have agreements in place to ensure that the elements within plans and procedures will be in effect at the time of an incident. The agreements should specify all of the communications systems and platforms through which the parties agree to use or share information.

4. EQUIPMENT STANDARDS AND TRAINING

Communications equipment used by emergency management/response personnel often consists of components and systems that may be connected through common interfaces, many of which rely on the private sector to provide their operational backbone. Public/private communication systems and associated equipment should be regularly enhanced and updated, as their maintenance is essential to effective emergency management and incident response activities. The wide range of conditions under which communications systems will be used should be considered when developing standards associated with the systems and equipment. Training and exercises that employ interoperable systems and equipment are necessary for personnel to understand their capabilities and limitations before an incident. In addition, the need for "hardened" laptops and/or personal digital assistants should be considered in the communications plan.

C. ORGANIZATION AND OPERATIONS

1. INCIDENT INFORMATION

During the course of an incident, information is vital to assist the IC, UC, and supporting agencies and organizations in making decisions. Much of the information is used for diverse functions within the Incident Command System. For example, the same piece of information may:

- Aid in the planning process to develop an Incident Action Plan (IAP).
- Be a key point in the release of public information.
- Assist the Finance/Administration Section in determining incident cost.
- Determine the need for additional involvement of NGO or private-sector resources.
- Identify a safety issue.
- Follow up on an information request.

The following are examples of information generated by an incident that can be used for decisionmaking purposes.

a. Incident Notification, Situation, and Status Reports

Incident reporting and documentation procedures should be standardized to ensure that situational awareness is maintained and that emergency management/response personnel have easy access to critical information. Situation reports offer a snapshot of the past operational period and contain confirmed or verified information regarding the explicit details (who, what, when, where, and how) relating to the incident. Status reports, which may be contained in situation reports, relay information specifically related to the status of resources (e.g., availability or assignment of resources).

The information contained in incident notification, situation, and status reports must be standardized in order to facilitate its processing; however, the standardization must not prevent the collection or dissemination of information unique to a reporting organization. Transmission of data in a common format enables the passing of pertinent information to appropriate jurisdictions and organizations and to a national system that can handle data queries and information/intelligence assessments and analysis.

b. Analytical Data

Data, such as information on public health and environmental monitoring, should be collected in a manner that observes standard data collection techniques and definitions. The data should then be transmitted using standardized analysis processes. During incidents that require public health and environmental sampling, multiple organizations at different levels of government often collect data, so standardization of data collection and analysis is critical. Additionally, standardization of sampling and data collection enables more reliable analysis and improves the quality of assessments provided to decisionmakers.

c. Geospatial Information

Geospatial information is defined as information pertaining to the geographic location and characteristics of natural or constructed features and boundaries. It is often used to integrate assessments, situation reports, and incident notification into a common operating picture and as a data fusion and analysis tool to synthesize many kinds and sources of data and imagery. The use of geospatial data (and the recognition of its intelligence capabilities) is increasingly important during incidents. Geospatial information capabilities (such as nationally consistent grid systems or global positioning systems based on lines of longitude and latitude) should be managed through preparedness efforts and integrated within the command, coordination, and support elements of an incident, including resource management and public information.

The use of geospatial data should be tied to consistent standards, as it has the potential to be misinterpreted, transposed incorrectly, or otherwise misapplied, causing inconspicuous yet serious errors. Standards covering geospatial information should also enable systems to be used in remote field locations or devastated areas where telecommunications may not be capable of handling large images or may be limited in terms of computing hardware.

2. COMMUNICATIONS STANDARDS AND FORMATS

Communications and data standards, related testing, and associated compliance mechanisms are necessary to enable diverse organizations to work together effectively. These include a standard set of organizational elements and functions, common "typing" of resources to reflect specific capabilities, and common identifiers for facilities and operational locations used to support incident operations.[13] Common terminology, standards, and procedures should be established and detailed in plans and agreements, where possible. Jurisdictions may be required to comply with national interoperable communications standards, once developed. Standards appropriate for NIMS users will be designated by the National Integration Center (NIC) in partnership with recognized standards development organizations.

a. Radio Usage Procedures

Procedures and protocols for incident-specific communications and other critical incident information should be set forth in agreements or plans prior to an incident, where possible. These procedures and protocols form the foundation for the development of the communications plan during an incident. The receiving center should be required to acknowledge receipt of the emergency information. Additionally, each agency/organization should be responsible for disseminating this information to its respective personnel.

> During incident response activities, radio traffic should be restricted to those messages necessary for the effective execution of emergency management/response personnel tasks.

All emergency management/response personnel participating in emergency management and incident response activities should follow recognized procedures and protocols for establishing interoperability, coordination, and command and control.

---

[13] See page 41, Component III: Resource Management, Identifying and Typing Resources.

b. Common Terminology, Plain Language (Clear Text), Compatibility

The ability of emergency management/response personnel from different disciplines, jurisdictions, organizations, and agencies to work together depends greatly on their ability to communicate with each other. Common terminology enables emergency management/response personnel to communicate clearly with one another and effectively coordinate activities, no matter the size, scope, location, or complexity of the incident.

The use of plain language (clear text) in emergency management and incident response is a matter of public safety, especially the safety of emergency management/response personnel and those affected by the incident. It is critical that all those involved with an incident know and use commonly established operational structures, terminology, policies, and procedures. This will facilitate interoperability across agencies/organizations, jurisdictions, and disciplines.

All communications between organizational elements during an incident, whether oral or written, should be in plain language; this ensures that information dissemination is timely, clear, acknowledged, and understood by all intended recipients. Codes should not be used, and all communications should be confined to essential messages. The use of acronyms should be avoided during incidents requiring the participation of multiple agencies or organizations. Policies and procedures that foster compatibility should be defined to allow information sharing among all emergency management/response personnel and their affiliated organizations to the greatest extent possible.

c. Encryption or Tactical Language

When necessary, emergency management/response personnel and their affiliated organizations need to have a methodology and the systems in place to encrypt information so that security can be maintained. Although plain language may be appropriate during response to most incidents, tactical language is occasionally warranted due to the nature of the incident (e.g., during an ongoing terrorist event). The use of specialized encryption and tactical language should be incorporated into any comprehensive IAP or incident management communications plan.

d. Joint Information System and Joint Information Center

The Joint Information System (JIS) and the Joint Information Center (JIC)[14] are designed to foster the use of common information formats. The JIS integrates incident information and public affairs into a cohesive organization designed to provide consistent, coordinated, accurate, accessible, and timely information during crisis or incident operations.

The JIC provides a structure for developing and delivering incident-related coordinated messages. It develops, recommends, and executes public information plans and strategies; advises the IC, UC, and supporting agencies or organizations concerning public affairs issues that could affect a response effort; and controls rumors and inaccurate information that could undermine public confidence in the emergency response effort. It is the central point of contact for all news media at the scene of an incident. Public information officials from all participating agencies/organizations should co-locate at the JIC.

---

[14] See pages 70–71, Component IV: Command and Management, Joint Information System and Joint Information Center.

e. Internet/Web Procedures

The Internet and other Web-based tools can be resources for emergency management/response personnel and their affiliated organizations. For example, these tools can be used prior to and during incidents as a mechanism to offer situational awareness to organizations/agencies involved in the incident or to the public, when appropriate.

> The Internet and other Web-based tools can be used, as appropriate, during incidents to help with situational awareness and crisis information management.

Procedures for use of these tools during an incident should be established to leverage them as valuable communications system resources. Information posted or shared during an incident through these applications should follow planned and standardized methods and generally conform with the overall standards, procedures, and protocols.

f. Information Security

Procedures and protocols must be established to ensure information security. Inadequate information security can result in the untimely, inappropriate, and piecemeal release of information, which increases the likelihood of misunderstanding and can compound already complicated public safety issues. The release of inappropriate classified or sensitive public health or law enforcement information can jeopardize national security, ongoing investigations, or public health. Misinformation can place persons in danger, cause public panic, and disrupt the critical flow of proper information. Correcting misinformation wastes the valuable time and effort of incident response personnel.

Individuals and organizations that have access to incident information and, in particular, contribute information to the system (e.g., situation reports) must be properly authenticated and certified for security purposes. This requires a national authentication and security certification standard that is flexible and robust enough to ensure that information can be properly authenticated and protected. Although the NIC is responsible for facilitating the development of these standards, all levels of government, NGOs, and the private sector should collaborate on the authentication process.

COMPONENT III: RESOURCE MANAGEMENT

Emergency management and incident response activities require carefully managed resources (personnel, teams, facilities, equipment, and/or supplies) to meet incident needs. Utilization of the standardized resource management concepts such as typing, inventorying, organizing, and tracking will facilitate the dispatch, deployment, and recovery of resources before, during, and after an incident. Resource management should be flexible and scalable in order to support any incident and be adaptable to changes. Efficient and effective deployment of resources requires that resource management concepts and principles be used in all phases of emergency management and incident response.

From routine, local incidents to incidents that require a coordinated Federal response, resource management involves the coordination, oversight, and processes that provide timely and appropriate resources during an incident. Resources may support on-scene and command operations through the Incident Command Post (ICP) or function within the Multiagency Coordination System(s)[15] (MACS) serving at an Emergency Operations Center (EOC) or similar site.

As incident priorities are established, needs are identified, and resources are ordered, resource management systems are used to process the resource requests. In the initial stages of an incident, most of the resources requested are addressed locally or through mutual aid agreements and/or assistance agreements. As an incident grows in size or complexity, or if it starts on a large scale, resource needs may be met by other sources. In a case of competition for critical resources, MACS may be used to prioritize and coordinate resource allocation and distribution according to resource availability, needs of other incidents, and other constraints and considerations.

> For certain kinds of incidents, resource needs may be anticipated well enough to develop a deployment strategy, incorporating all elements of resource management.
>
> - **Preincident assignment:** Assigning personnel and teams to specific tasks in anticipation of incident response
> - **"Move-up" or "backfill" strategy:** Moving resources nearest to an incident into the incident area, with more distant resources filling the void by backfilling behind the deploying resources
> - **Regional pre-positioning of resources:** Using designated areas for final preparation of resources prior to mobilization and for recovery of resources during demobilization

---

[15] See page 64, Component IV: Command and Management, for more information on MACS.

A. CONCEPTS AND PRINCIPLES

1. CONCEPTS

The underlying concepts of resource management are as follows:

- **Consistency:** Provision of a standard method for identifying, acquiring, allocating, and tracking resources.
- **Standardization:** Resource classification to improve the effectiveness of mutual aid agreements or assistance agreements.
- **Coordination:** Facilitation and integration of resources for optimal benefit.
- **Use:** Incorporating available resources from all levels of government, nongovernmental organizations (NGOs), and the private sector, where appropriate, in a jurisdiction's resource management planning efforts.
- **Information Management:** Provisions for the thorough integration of communications and information management elements into resource management organizations, processes, technologies, and decision support.
- **Credentialing:** Use of criteria that ensure consistent training, licensure, and certification standards.

2. PRINCIPLES

The foundations of resource management are based on the following five interwoven principles.

a. Planning

Coordinated planning, training to common standards, and inclusive exercises provide a foundation for the interoperability and compatibility of resources throughout an incident. Jurisdictions should work together in advance of an incident to develop plans for identifying, ordering, managing, and employing resources. The planning process should include identifying resource needs based on the threats to and vulnerabilities of the jurisdiction and developing alternative strategies to obtain the needed resources.

Planning may include the creation of new policies to encourage positioning of resources near the expected incident site in response to anticipated resource needs. Plans should anticipate conditions or circumstances that may trigger a specific reaction, such as the restocking of supplies when inventories reach a predetermined minimum. Organizations and jurisdictions should continually assess the status of their resources in order to have an accurate list of resources available at any given time. Additionally, emergency Management/response personnel[16] should be familiar with the *National Response Framework* and should be prepared to integrate and/or coordinate with Federal resources.

---

[16] Emergency management/response personnel include Federal, State, territorial, tribal, substate regional, and local governments, nongovernmental organizations, private-sector organizations, critical infrastructure owners and operators, and all other organizations and individuals who assume an emergency management role.

b. Use of Agreements

Agreements among all parties providing or requesting resources are necessary to enable effective and efficient resource management during incident operations. This includes developing and maintaining standing agreements and contracts for services and supplies that may be needed during an incident.

c. Categorizing Resources

Resources are organized by category, kind, and type, including size, capacity, capability, skill, and other characteristics. This makes the resource-ordering and dispatch process within and across jurisdictions, and among all levels of governments, NGOs, and the private sector, more efficient and ensures that needed resources are received.

d. Resource Identification and Ordering

The resource management process uses standardized methods to identify, order, mobilize, and track the resources required to support incident management activities. Those with resource management responsibilities perform these tasks either at the request of the Incident Commander (IC) or in accordance with planning requirements. Identification and ordering of resources are intertwined. In some cases, the identification and ordering process is compressed, where an IC has determined the resources necessary for the task and specifies a resource order directly. However, in larger, more complex incidents, the IC may not be fully aware of resources available. At this point, the IC may identify needs based on incident objectives and use the resource management process to fill these needs.

e. Effective Management of Resources

Resource management involves acquisition procedures, management information, and redundant systems and protocols for ordering, mobilizing, dispatching, and demobilizing resources.

(1) Acquisition Procedures

Acquisition procedures are used to obtain resources to support operational requirements. Examples include mission tasking, contracting, drawing from existing stocks, and making small purchases. A key aspect of the inventorying process is determining whether an organization needs to warehouse specific items prior to an incident. Material resources may be acquired in advance and stockpiled or obtained "just in time" through appropriate preincident contracts. Those with resource management responsibilities make this decision by considering the urgency of the need, whether sufficient quantities of required items are on hand, and whether the required items can be produced quickly enough to meet demand.

> **Stockpiling vs. Just in Time**
>
> Resources may be acquired in advance and stored in a warehouse (i.e., stockpiled) or supplied "just in time," typically using a preincident contract. Planning and resource accounting procedures should accommodate both types of resource supply.

Another important part of the process is managing inventories with shelf-life or special maintenance considerations. Strict reliance on stockpiling raises issues concerning shelf life and durability; however, strict reliance on "just in time" resources raises its own concerns related to timely delivery. Assets that are counted on for "just in time" need to be accurately accounted for to ensure that multiple jurisdictions or private-sector organizations are not relying solely on the same response asset, which can lead to shortages during a response. Those with resource management responsibilities should build sufficient funding into their budgets for periodic replenishments, preventive maintenance, and capital improvements. An integral part of acquisition procedures is developing methods and protocols for the handling and distribution of donated resources.

(2) Management Information Systems

These systems are used to provide decision support information to managers by collecting, updating, and processing data, and tracking resources. They enhance resource status information flow and provide real-time data in a fast-paced environment where different jurisdictions, emergency management/response personnel, and their affiliated organizations are managing different aspects of the incident and should coordinate their efforts. Examples of management information systems include resource tracking, transportation tracking, inventory management, reporting, and geographical information systems. The selection and use of systems for resource management should be based on the identification of the information needs within a jurisdiction.

(3) Redundant Information Systems

Those with resource management responsibilities should be able to identify and activate backup systems to manage resources in the event that the primary resource management information system is disrupted or unavailable. Management information systems should also have sufficiently redundant and diverse power supplies and communication capabilities. If possible, the backup storage should not be co-located, and the information should be backed up at least every 24 hours during the incident.

(4) Ordering, Mobilization, and Demobilization Protocols

Protocols are followed when requesting resources, prioritizing requests, activating and mobilizing resources to incidents, and returning resources to normal status. Preparedness organizations develop standard protocols for use within their jurisdictions. Examples include tracking systems that identify the location and status of mobilized or dispatched resources, and procedures to demobilize resources and return them to their original locations and status.

B. MANAGING RESOURCES

To implement these concepts and principles in the primary tasks of resource management, NIMS includes standardized procedures, methodologies, and functions in its seven-step resource management process. This process reflects functional considerations, geographic factors, and validated practices within and across disciplines and is continually adjusted as new lessons are learned.

Resource maintenance is important throughout all aspects of resource management. Maintenance prior to resource deployment ensures availability and capability. Maintenance during the deployment phase ensures continued capabilities, such as adequate fuel supplies during use. Postoperational inspection and maintenance ensures future availability.

COMPONENT III: RESOURCE MANAGEMENT

The foundation for resource management provided in this component will be expanded and refined over time in a collaborative cross-jurisdictional, cross-disciplinary effort led by the National Integration Center (NIC).

The resource management process can be separated into two parts: resource management as an element of preparedness and resource management during an incident. The preparedness activities (resource typing, credentialing, and inventorying) are conducted on a continual basis to help ensure that resources are ready to be mobilized when called to an incident. Resource management during an incident is a finite process, as shown in Figure 1, with a distinct beginning and ending specific to the needs of the particular incident.

Figure 1. Resource Management During an Incident

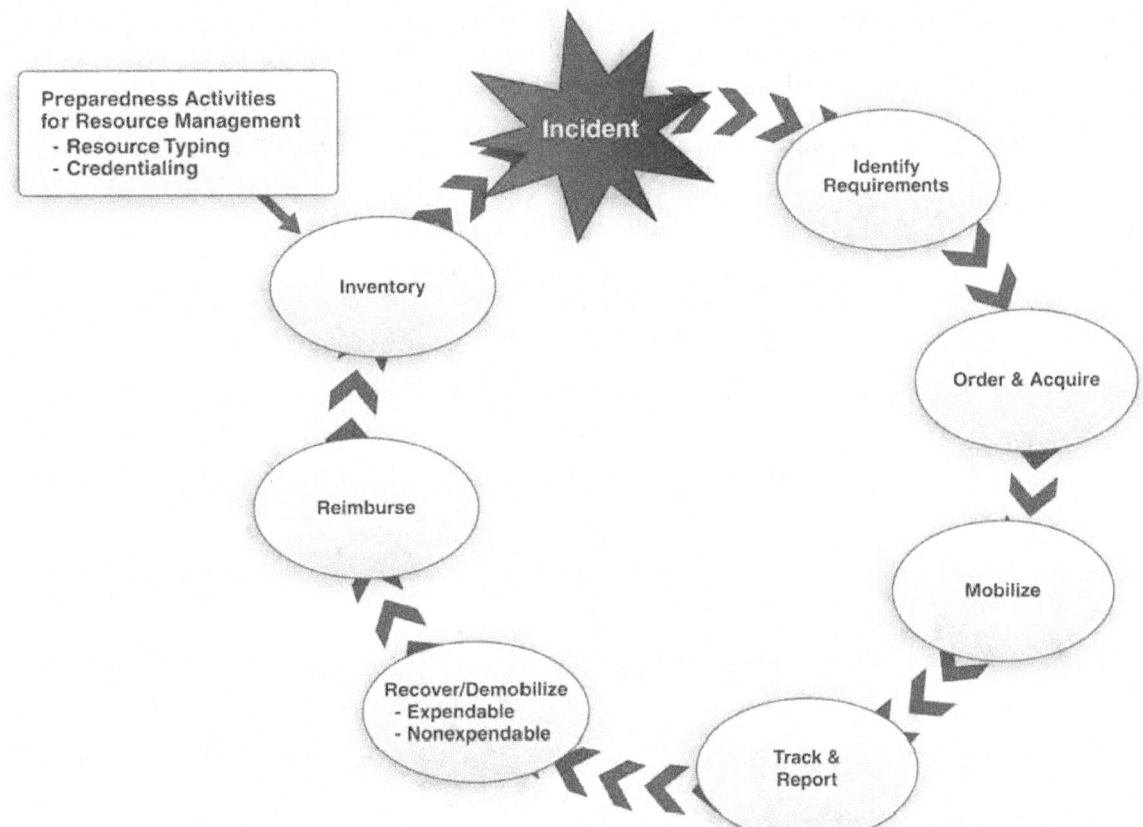

1. IDENTIFY REQUIREMENTS

When an incident occurs, those with resource management responsibilities should continually identify, refine, and validate resource requirements. This process involves accurately identifying what and how much is needed, where and when it is needed, and who will be receiving or using it. Resources to be identified in this way include equipment, supplies, facilities, and personnel or emergency response teams. If a requestor is unable to describe an item by resource type or classification, those with resource management responsibilities should provide technical advice to enable the requirements to be defined and translated into a specification. Specific resources for critical infrastructure and key resources may need to be identified and coordinated through mutual aid agreements or assistance agreements unique to those sectors, and should be accessible through preparedness organizations and/or MACS.

Resource availability and requirements will constantly change as the incident evolves. Consequently, all emergency management/response personnel and their affiliated organizations participating in an operation should coordinate closely throughout this process. Coordination should begin as early as possible, preferably prior to the need for incident response activities.

In instances when an incident is projected to have catastrophic implications (e.g., a major hurricane or flooding), States and/or the Federal Government may position resources in the anticipated incident area. In cases where there is time to assess the requirements and plan for a catastrophic incident, the Federal response will be coordinated with State, tribal, and local jurisdictions, and the positioning of Federal resources will be tailored to address the specific situation. The flow of requests and assistance is shown in Figure 2.

Figure 2. Flow of Requests and Assistance During Large-Scale Incidents

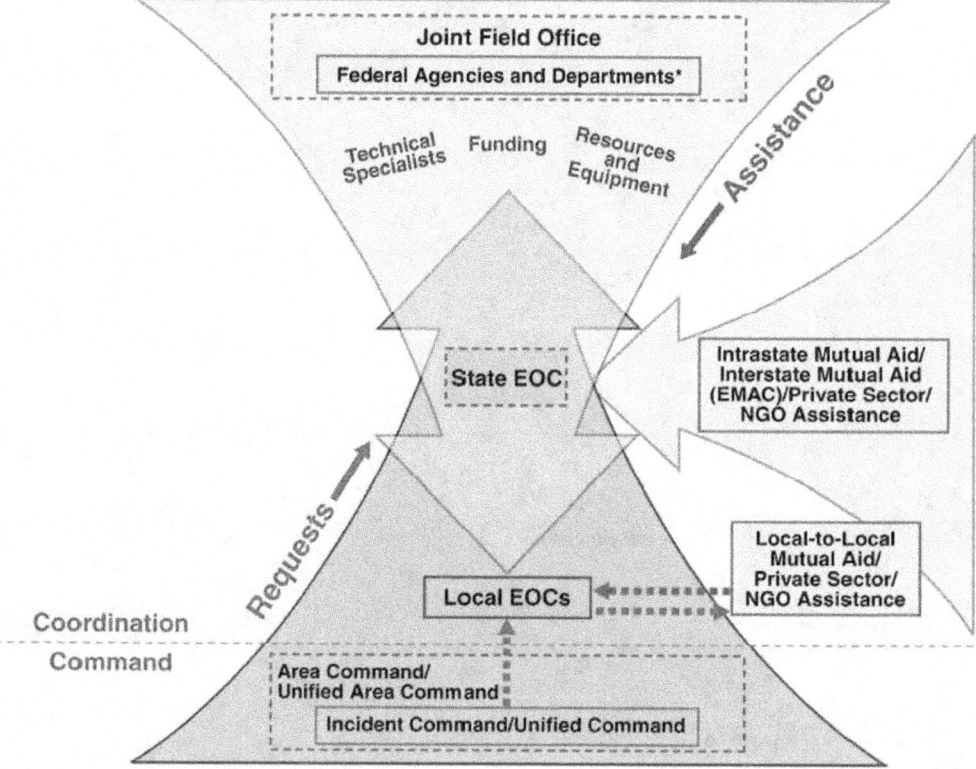

*Some Federal agencies (U.S. Coast Guard, Environmental Protection Agency, etc.) have statutory responsibility for response and may coordinate and/or integrate directly with affected jurisdictions.

2. ORDER AND ACQUIRE

Requests for resources that cannot be obtained locally are submitted using standardized resource-ordering procedures. These requests are generally forwarded first to an adjacent locality or substate region and then to the State.

The decision cycles for placing and filling resource orders are different for field/incident personnel with resource management responsibilities and resource coordination processes such as MACS. The IC will develop resource requests based on priorities that consider current and successive operational periods. Decisions about resource allocation are based on organization or agency protocol and possibly the resource demands of other incidents. Requested resources will be mobilized only with the consent of the jurisdiction that is being asked to provide the resources. Discrepancies between requested resources and those available for delivery must be communicated to the requestor.

> **Avoid Bypassing Systems**
>
> All of those with responsibilities for managing resources, including public officials, should recognize the limitations inherent in requesting resources by circumventing the official resource coordination process within the multiagency coordination system supporting the incident(s). These requests do not proceed within the context of orderly resource management systems, and typically lead to inefficient use and/or lack of accounting of resources.

3. MOBILIZE

Emergency management/response personnel begin mobilizing when notified through established channels. At the time of notification, they are given the date, time, and place of departure; mode of transportation to the incident; estimated date and time of arrival; reporting location (address, contact name, and phone number); anticipated incident assignment; anticipated duration of deployment; resource order number; incident number; and applicable cost and funding codes. The resource-tracking and mobilization processes are directly linked. When resources arrive on scene, they must be formally checked in. This starts the on-scene check-in process and validates the order requirements. Notification that the resources have arrived is made through the appropriate channels.

The mobilization process may include deployment planning based on existing interagency mobilization guidelines; equipping; training; designating assembly points that have facilities suitable for logistical support; and obtaining transportation to deliver resources to the incident most quickly, in line with priorities and budgets. Mobilization plans should also recognize that some resources are fixed facilities, such as laboratories, hospitals, EOCs, shelters, and waste management systems. These facilities assist operations without moving into the incident area in the way that other resources are mobilized. Plans and systems to monitor resource mobilization status should be flexible enough to adapt to both types of mobilization.

Managers should plan and prepare for the demobilization process at the same time that they begin the resource mobilization process. Early planning for demobilization facilitates accountability and makes the transportation of resources as efficient as possible—in terms of both costs and time of delivery.

4. TRACK AND REPORT

Resource tracking is a standardized, integrated process conducted prior to, during, and after an incident by all emergency management/response personnel and their affiliated organizations, as appropriate. This process provides a clear picture of where resources are located; helps staff prepare to receive resources; protects the safety and security of equipment, supplies, and personnel; and enables their coordination and movement. Those with resource management responsibilities use established procedures to track resources continuously from mobilization through demobilization. Managers should follow all procedures for acquiring and managing resources, including reconciliation, accounting, auditing, and inventorying.

5. RECOVER AND DEMOBILIZE

Recovery involves the final disposition of all resources, including those located at the incident site and at fixed facilities. During this process, resources are rehabilitated, replenished, disposed of, and/or retrograded.

Demobilization is the orderly, safe, and efficient return of an incident resource to its original location and status. It can begin at any point of an incident, but should begin as soon as possible to facilitate accountability. The demobilization process should coordinate between incident(s) and MACS to reassign resources, if necessary, and to prioritize critical resource needs during demobilization.

The Demobilization Unit in the Planning Section develops an Incident Demobilization Plan, containing specific demobilization instructions, as part of the Incident Action Plan. Demobilization planning and processes should include provisions addressing the safe return of resources to their original location and status, and notification of return. Demobilization should also include processes for tracking resources and for addressing applicable reimbursement. Furthermore, documentation regarding the transportation of resources should be collected and maintained for reimbursement, if applicable. Demobilization provisions may need to meet specific organizational requirements.

a. Nonexpendable Resources

Nonexpendable resources (such as personnel, fire engines, and durable equipment) are fully accounted for both during the incident and when they are returned to the providing organization. The organization then restores the resources to fully functional capability and readies them for the next mobilization. Broken or lost items should be replaced through the appropriate resupply process by the organization with invoicing responsibility for the incident, or as defined in existing agreements. It is critical that fixed-facility resources also be restored to their full functional capability in order to ensure readiness for the next mobilization. In the case of human resources, such as Incident Management Teams, adequate rest and recuperation time and facilities should be provided. Important occupational health and mental health issues should also be addressed, including monitoring the immediate and long-term effects of the incident (chronic and acute) on emergency management/response personnel.

b. Expendable Resources

Expendable resources, such as water, food, fuel, and other one-time-use supplies, must be fully accounted for. The incident management organization bears the costs of expendable resources, as authorized in financial agreements executed by preparedness organizations. Restocking occurs at the point from which a resource was issued. Returned resources that are not in restorable condition, whether expendable or nonexpendable, must be declared as excess according to established regulations and policies of the controlling jurisdiction, agency, or organization. Waste management is of special note in the process of recovering resources, as resources that require special handling and disposition (e.g., biological waste and contaminated supplies, debris, and equipment) are handled according to established regulations and policies.

6. REIMBURSE

Reimbursement provides a mechanism to recoup funds expended for incident-specific activities. Processes for reimbursement play an important role in establishing and maintaining the readiness of resources and should be in place to ensure that resource providers are reimbursed in a timely manner. They should include mechanisms for collecting bills, validating costs against the scope of the work, ensuring that proper authorities are involved, and accessing reimbursement programs. Reimbursement mechanisms should be included in preparedness plans, mutual aid agreements, and assistance agreements. Some resources rendered may or may not be reimbursed, based on agreements established before the incident.

7. INVENTORY

Resource management uses various resource inventory systems to assess the availability of assets provided by jurisdictions. Preparedness organizations should inventory and maintain current data on their available resources. The data are then made available to communications/dispatch centers and EOCs and organizations within MACS. Resources identified within an inventory system are not an indication of automatic availability. The jurisdiction and/or owner of the resources has the final determination on availability.

Inventory systems for resource management should be adaptable and scalable and should account for the potential of double-counting personnel and/or equipment. In particular, resource summaries should clearly reflect any overlap of personnel across different resource pools. Personnel inventories should reflect single resources with multiple skills, taking care not to overstate the total resources. For example, many firefighters also have credentials as emergency medical technicians (EMTs). A resource summary, then, could count a firefighter as a firefighter or as an EMT, but not as both. The total should reflect the number of available personnel, not simply the sum of the firefighter and EMT counts.

Deployable resources have different inventory, ordering, and response profiles depending on their primary use during the response or recovery phases of an incident. Planning for resource use, inventory, and tracking should recognize the fundamental difference in resource deployment in the response and recovery phases. The response phase relies heavily on mutual aid agreements and assistance agreements, while recovery resources are typically acquired through contracts with NGOs and/or the private sector.

COMPONENT III: RESOURCE MANAGEMENT

a. Credentialing

The credentialing process entails the objective evaluation and documentation of an individual's current certification, license, or degree; training and experience; and competence or proficiency to meet nationally accepted standards, provide particular services and/or functions, or perform specific tasks under specific conditions during an incident.

For the purpose of NIMS, credentialing is the administrative process for validating personnel qualifications and providing authorization to perform specific functions and to have specific access to an incident involving mutual aid.

Figure 3 illustrates the following NIC-recommended process for credentialing under NIMS:

When a request for mutual aid is received, the potential supporting department or agency evaluates its capacity to accommodate the anticipated loss of the resources that would be deployed without compromising mission performance (e.g., can a fire department allow 20 percent of its equipment and personnel to be deployed to another jurisdiction for 30 days and still meet its own community's needs?).

If the potential supporting department or agency determines that it can accommodate the requested deployment of resources, it must next identify specific personnel who will be deployed. The department or agency then submits applications for each member selected for deployment to an authorized accrediting agency identified by the credentialing authority of the State to which the mutual aid will be provided.

The accrediting agency evaluates each application and determines whether the applicant meets the established criteria for the positions required by the mission. Applications that the authorized accrediting agency determines fail to meet established criteria are returned to the submitting department or agency, and may be resubmitted with additional documentation or when the applicant's qualifications change. For applications that are approved by the authorized accrediting agency, the following steps are taken:

- The applicant's department or agency is notified.
- A record is created on the individual in the official credentialing database.
- An identification card or other credential is issued to the individual. (The identification card or credential should include an expiration date and be reissued as appropriate.)
- Information on the applicant is uploaded to the incident management infrastructure.

While credentialing includes the issuing of identification cards or credentials, it is separate and distinct from the incident badging process. When access to a site is controlled through special badging, the badging process must be based on verification of identity, qualifications, and deployment authorization.

Organizations utilizing volunteers, especially spontaneous volunteers, are responsible for ensuring each volunteer's eligibility to participate in a response. These organizations— governmental agencies responsible for coordinating emergency responses, volunteer management agencies (e.g., Red Cross, Emergency System for Advance Registration of Volunteer Health Professionals, Medical Reserve Corps, etc.), and other potential users of volunteers (e.g., hospitals, fire and police departments, etc.)—must develop protocols governing the activation and use of volunteers. Careful coordination is required to ensure the provision of services is not hindered by unaddressed safety and security considerations or legal or regulatory issues.

Figure 3. Recommended NIMS Personnel Credentialing Process

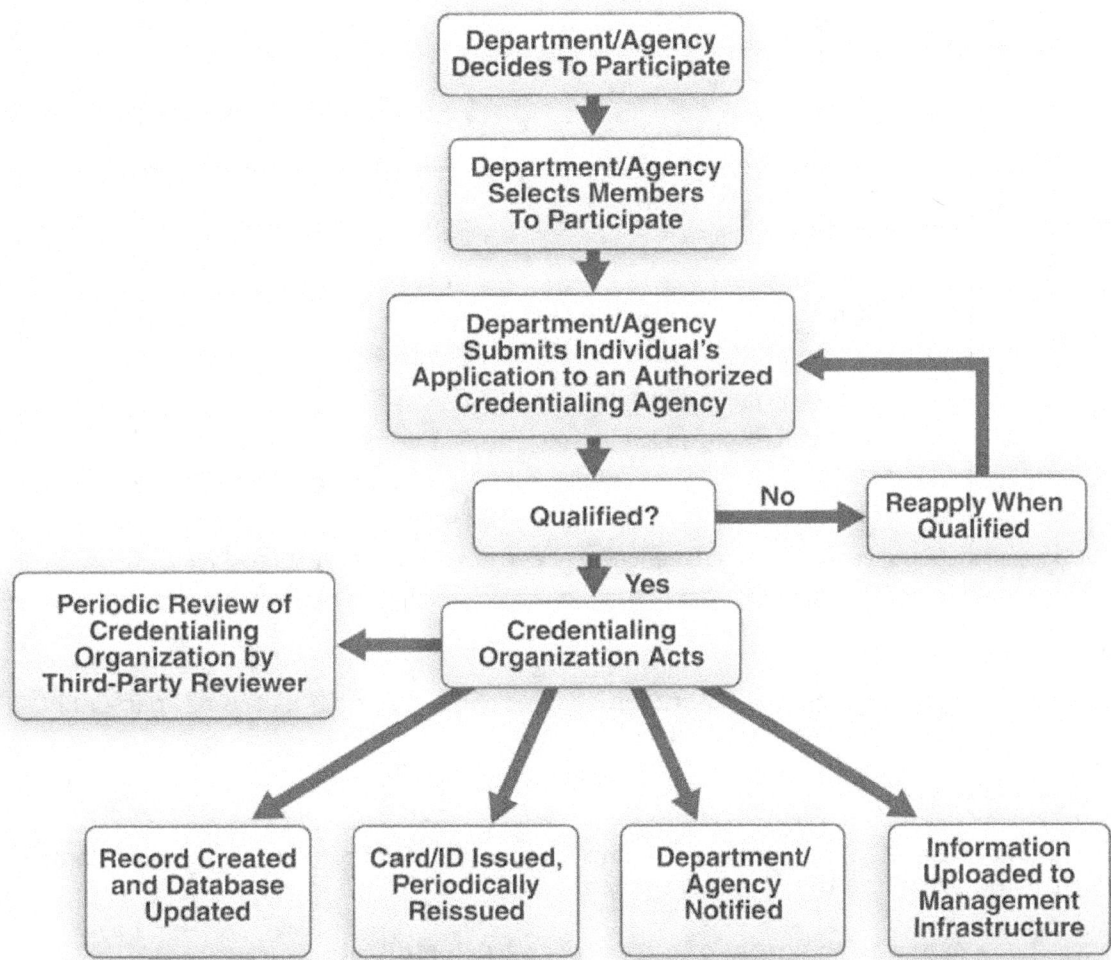

b. Identifying and Typing Resources

Resource typing is categorizing, by capability, the resources requested, deployed, and used in incidents.[17] Measurable standards identifying resource capabilities and performance levels serve as the basis for categories. Resource users at all levels use these standards to identify and inventory resources. Resource kinds may be divided into subcategories to define more precisely the capabilities needed to meet specific requirements. Resource typing is a continuous process designed to be as simple as possible; it facilitates frequent use and accuracy in obtaining needed resources. To allow resources to be deployed and used on a national basis, the NIC (with input from Federal, State, tribal, local, private-

---

[17] See pages 83–87, Appendix A, for more information on resource typing.

sector, nongovernmental, and national professional organizations) is responsible for facilitating the development and issuance of national standards for resource typing and ensuring that these typed resources reflect operational capabilities.[18]

(1) Category

This is the function for which a resource would be most useful. Table 2 lists examples of categories used in a national resource-typing protocol.

Table 2. Example Categories for National Resource Typing

• Transportation	• Health and medical
• Communications	• Search and rescue
• Public works and engineering	• Hazardous materials response
• Firefighting	• Food and water
• Information and planning	• Energy
• Law enforcement and security	• Public information
• Mass care	• Animals and agricultural issues
• Resource management	• Volunteers and donations

(2) Kind

Kind refers to broad classes that characterize like resources, such as teams, personnel, equipment, supplies, vehicles, and aircraft.

(a) Components

Components are the elements that make up a resource. For example, an engine company may be listed as having the eight components shown in Table 3.

**Table 3. Example of a Resource With Multiple Components
(Firefighting Engine Company)**

(1) Pump	(5) Water tank
(2) Hose 2½"	(6) Ladder
(3) Hose 1¾"	(7) Master stream
(4) Hand tools	(8) Personnel

---

[18] Proposals for additions to the NIMS Typed Resources Definitions may be submitted to the NIC, Incident Management Systems Division, for consideration.

As another example, urban search and rescue teams consist of two 31-person teams, four canines, and a comprehensive equipment cache. The cache is divided into five separate color-coded elements and is stored in containers that meet specific requirements.

(b) Measures

Measures are standards that identify capability and/or capacity. The specific measures used will depend on the kind of resource being typed and the mission envisioned. Measures must be useful in describing a resource's capability to support the mission. As an example, one measure for a disaster medical assistance team is the number of patients it can care for per day. An appropriate measure for a hose might be the number of gallons of water per hour that can flow through it.

(3) Type

Type refers to the level of resource capability. Assigning the Type 1 label to a resource implies that it has a greater level of capability than a Type 2 of the same resource (for example, due to its power, size, or capacity), and so on to Type 4. Typing provides managers with additional information to aid in the selection and best use of resources. In some cases, a resource may have fewer than or more than four types; in such cases, either additional types will be identified, or the type will be described as "not applicable." The type assigned to a resource or a component is based on a minimum level of capability described by the identified measure(s) for that resource. For example, the U.S. Coast Guard has typed oil skimmers based on barrels per day, as outlined in Table 4.

Table 4. Example of a Resource With Multiple Types
(Coast Guard Oil Skimmer)

Type 1	9,600 bbls/day	Type 3	480 bbls/day
Type 2	2,880 bbls/day	Type 4	N/A

(4) Additional Information

The national resource-typing protocol will also provide the capability to use additional information that is pertinent to resource decisionmaking. For example, if a particular set of resources can be released to support an incident only under particular authorities or laws, the protocol should alert responsible parties to such limitations.

COMPONENT IV:
COMMAND AND MANAGEMENT

The NIMS components discussed previously—Preparedness, Communications and Information Management, and Resource Management—provide a framework to facilitate clear response authority, resource acquisition, and effective management during incident response. The Incident Command System (ICS), Multiagency Coordination System (MACS), and Public Information are the fundamental elements of incident management. These elements provide standardization through consistent terminology and established organizational structures. Emergency management and incident response refer to the broad spectrum of activities and organizations providing effective and efficient operations, coordination, and support. Incident management, by distinction, includes directing specific incident operations; acquiring, coordinating, and delivering resources to incident sites; and sharing information about the incident with the public. Taken together, these elements of Command and Management are the most visible aspects of incident management, typically executed with a sense of urgency. This component describes the systems used to facilitate incident Command and Management operations.

A. INCIDENT COMMAND SYSTEM

Most incidents are managed locally and are typically handled by local communications/ dispatch centers and emergency management/response personnel[19] within a single jurisdiction. The majority of responses need go no further. In other instances, incidents that begin with a single response within a single jurisdiction rapidly expand to multidisciplinary, multijurisdictional levels requiring significant additional resources and operational support. ICS provides a flexible core mechanism for coordinated and collaborative incident management, whether for incidents where additional resources are required or are provided from different organizations within a single jurisdiction or outside the jurisdiction, or for complex incidents with national implications (such as an emerging infectious disease or a bioterrorism attack). When a single incident covers a large geographical area, multiple local emergency management and incident response agencies may be required. The responding "agencies" are defined as the governmental agencies, though in certain circumstances nongovernmental organizations (NGOs) and private-sector organizations may be included. Effective cross-jurisdictional coordination using processes and systems is absolutely critical in this situation.

ICS is a widely applicable management system designed to enable effective, efficient incident management by integrating a combination of facilities, equipment, personnel, procedures, and communications operating within a common organizational structure. ICS is a fundamental form of management established in a standard format, with the purpose of enabling incident managers to identify the key concerns associated with the incident—often under urgent conditions—without sacrificing attention to any component of the command system.

---

[19] Emergency management/response personnel include Federal, State, territorial, tribal, substate regional, and local governments, nongovernmental organizations, private-sector organizations, critical infrastructure owners and operators, and all other organizations and individuals who assume an emergency management role.

ICS is used to organize on-scene operations for a broad spectrum of emergencies from small to complex incidents, both natural and manmade. The field response level is where emergency management/response personnel, under the command of an appropriate authority, carry out tactical decisions and activities in direct response to an incident or threat. Resources from the Federal, State, tribal, or local levels, when appropriately deployed, become part of the field ICS as prescribed by the local authority.

As a system, ICS is extremely useful; not only does it provide an organizational structure for incident management, but it also guides the process for planning, building, and adapting that structure. Using ICS for every incident or planned event helps hone and maintain skills needed for the large-scale incidents.

ICS is used by all levels of government—Federal, State, tribal, and local—as well as by many NGOs and the private sector. ICS is also applicable across disciplines. It is normally structured to facilitate activities in five major functional areas: Command, Operations, Planning, Logistics, and Finance/Administration. Intelligence/Investigations is an optional sixth functional area that is activated on a case-by-case basis.

Acts of biological, chemical, radiological, and nuclear terrorism may present unique challenges for the traditional ICS structure. Incidents that are not site specific, are geographically dispersed, or evolve over longer periods of time will require extraordinary coordination among all participants, including Federal, State, tribal, and local governments, as well as NGOs and the private sector.

1. MANAGEMENT CHARACTERISTICS

ICS is based on 14 proven management characteristics, each of which contributes to the strength and efficiency of the overall system.

a. Common Terminology

ICS establishes common terminology that allows diverse incident management and support organizations to work together across a wide variety of incident management functions and hazard scenarios. This common terminology covers the following:

(1) Organizational Functions

Major functions and functional units with incident management responsibilities are named and defined. Terminology for the organizational elements is standard and consistent.

(2) Resource Descriptions

Major resources—including personnel, facilities, and major equipment and supply items—that support incident management activities are given common names and are "typed" with respect to their capabilities, to help avoid confusion and to enhance interoperability.[20]

(3) Incident Facilities

Common terminology is used to designate the facilities in the vicinity of the incident area that will be used during the course of the incident.

---

[20] See page 41, Component III, Resource Management, Identifying and Typing Resources.

b. Modular Organization

The ICS organizational structure develops in a modular fashion based on the size and complexity of the incident, as well as the specifics of the hazard environment created by the incident. When needed, separate functional elements can be established, each of which may be further subdivided to enhance internal organizational management and external coordination. Responsibility for the establishment and expansion of the ICS modular organization ultimately rests with Incident Command, which bases the ICS organization on the requirements of the situation. As incident complexity increases, the organization expands from the top down as functional responsibilities are delegated. Concurrently with structural expansion, the number of management and supervisory positions expands to address the requirements of the incident adequately.

c. Management by Objectives

Management by objectives is communicated throughout the entire ICS organization and includes:

- Establishing incident objectives.
- Developing strategies based on incident objectives.
- Developing and issuing assignments, plans, procedures, and protocols.
- Establishing specific, measurable tactics or tasks for various incident management functional activities, and directing efforts to accomplish them, in support of defined strategies.
- Documenting results to measure performance and facilitate corrective actions.

d. Incident Action Planning

Centralized, coordinated incident action planning should guide all response activities. An Incident Action Plan (IAP) provides a concise, coherent means of capturing and communicating the overall incident priorities, objectives, strategies, and tactics in the context of both operational and support activities.

Every incident must have an action plan. However, not all incidents require written plans. The need for written plans and attachments is based on the requirements of the incident and the decision of the Incident Commander (IC) or Unified Command (UC). Most initial response operations are not captured with a formal IAP. However, if an incident is likely to extend beyond one operational period, become more complex, or involve multiple jurisdictions and/or agencies, preparing a written IAP will become increasingly important to maintain effective, efficient, and safe operations.

e. Manageable Span of Control

Span of control is key to effective and efficient incident management. Supervisors must be able to adequately supervise and control their subordinates, as well as communicate with and manage all resources under their supervision. The type of incident, nature of the task, hazards and safety factors, and distances between personnel and resources all influence span-of-control considerations.

> **Examples of Manageable Span of Control**
>
> In ICS, the span of control of any individual with incident management supervisory responsibility should range from 3 to 7 subordinates, with 5 being optimal. During a large-scale law enforcement operation, 8 to 10 subordinates may be optimal.

f. Incident Facilities and Locations

Various types of operational support facilities are established in the vicinity of an incident, depending on its size and complexity, to accomplish a variety of purposes. The IC will direct the identification and location of facilities based on the requirements of the situation. Typically designated facilities include Incident Command Posts, Bases, Camps, Staging Areas, mass casualty triage areas, point-of-distribution sites, and others as required.

g. Comprehensive Resource Management

Maintaining an accurate and up-to-date picture of resource utilization is a critical component of incident management and emergency response. Resources to be identified in this way include personnel, teams, equipment, supplies, and facilities available or potentially available for assignment or allocation. Resource management is described in detail in Component III.

h. Integrated Communications

Incident communications are facilitated through the development and use of a common communications plan and interoperable communications processes and architectures. The ICS 205 form is available to assist in developing a common communications plan. This integrated approach links the operational and support units of the various agencies involved and is necessary to maintain communications connectivity and discipline and to enable common situational awareness and interaction. Preparedness planning should address the equipment, systems, and protocols necessary to achieve integrated voice and data communications.

i. Establishment and Transfer of Command

The command function must be clearly established from the beginning of incident operations. The agency with primary jurisdictional authority over the incident designates the individual at the scene responsible for establishing command. When command is transferred, the process must include a briefing that captures all essential information for continuing safe and effective operations.

j. Chain of Command and Unity of Command

Chain of command refers to the orderly line of authority within the ranks of the incident management organization. Unity of command means that all individuals have a designated supervisor to whom they report at the scene of the incident. These principles clarify reporting relationships and eliminate the confusion caused by multiple, conflicting directives. Incident managers at all levels must be able to direct the actions of all personnel under their supervision.[21]

---

[21] Concepts of "command" and "unity of command" have distinct legal meanings for military forces and operations. For military forces, command runs from the President to the Secretary of Defense to the Commander of the combatant command to the commander of the forces. The "Unified Command" concept utilized by civil authorities is distinct from the military chain of command.

k. Unified Command

In incidents involving multiple jurisdictions, a single jurisdiction with multiagency involvement, or multiple jurisdictions with multiagency involvement, Unified Command allows agencies with different legal, geographic, and functional authorities and responsibilities to work together effectively without affecting individual agency authority, responsibility, or accountability.

l. Accountability

Effective accountability of resources at all jurisdictional levels and within individual functional areas during incident operations is essential. To that end, Check-In/Check-Out, Incident Action Planning, Unity of Command, Personal Responsibility, Span of Control, and Resource Tracking are the principles of accountability, which must be adhered to.[22]

m. Dispatch/Deployment

Resources should respond only when requested or when dispatched by an appropriate authority through established resource management systems. Resources not requested must refrain from spontaneous deployment to avoid overburdening the recipient and compounding accountability challenges.

n. Information and Intelligence Management

The incident management organization must establish a process for gathering, analyzing, assessing, sharing, and managing incident-related information and intelligence.

2. INCIDENT COMMAND AND COMMAND STAFF

Incident Command is responsible for overall management of the incident. Overall management includes Command Staff assignments required to support the command function. The Command and General Staffs are typically located at the Incident Command Post (ICP).

a. Incident Command

The command function may be conducted in one of two general ways:

(1) Single Incident Commander

When an incident occurs within a single jurisdiction and there is no jurisdictional or functional agency overlap, a single IC should be designated with overall incident management responsibility by the appropriate jurisdictional authority. (In some cases where incident management crosses jurisdictional and/or functional agency boundaries, a single IC may be designated if agreed upon.) Jurisdictions should consider designating ICs for established Incident Management Teams (IMTs).

---

[22] The principles of accountability are individually defined in the glossary.

The designated IC will develop the incident objectives on which subsequent incident action planning will be based. The IC will approve the IAP and all requests pertaining to ordering and releasing incident resources.

(2) Unified Command

UC is an important element in multijurisdictional or multiagency incident management. It provides guidelines to enable agencies with different legal, geographic, and functional responsibilities to coordinate, plan, and interact effectively. As a team effort, UC allows all agencies with jurisdictional authority or functional responsibility for the incident to jointly provide management direction through a common set of incident objectives and strategies and a single IAP. Each participating agency maintains its authority, responsibility, and accountability.

UC functions as a single integrated management organization, which involves:

- Co-located command at the ICP.
- One Operations Section Chief to direct tactical efforts.
- A coordinated process for resource ordering.
- Shared planning, logistical, and finance/administration functions, wherever possible.
- Coordinated approval of information releases.

> **Advantages of Using Unified Command**
>
> - A single set of objectives is developed for the entire incident.
> - A collective approach is used to develop strategies to achieve incident objectives.
> - Information flow and coordination are improved between all jurisdictions and agencies involved in the incident.
> - All agencies with responsibility for the incident have an understanding of joint priorities and restrictions.
> - No agency's legal authorities will be compromised or neglected.
> - The combined efforts of all agencies are optimized as they perform their respective assignments under a single IAP.

All agencies in the UC structure contribute to the process of:

- Selecting objectives.
- Determining overall incident strategies.
- Ensuring that joint planning for tactical activities is accomplished in accordance with approved incident objectives.
- Ensuring the integration of tactical operations.
- Approving, committing, and making optimum use of all assigned resources.

The exact composition of the UC structure will depend on the location(s) of the incident (i.e., which geographical jurisdictions or organizations are involved) and the type of incident (i.e., which functional agencies of the involved jurisdiction(s) or organization(s) are required). The designation of a single IC for some multijurisdictional incidents, if planned for in advance, may be considered in order to promote greater unity of effort and efficiency.

COMPONENT IV: COMMAND AND MANAGEMENT

The designated agency officials participating in the UC represent different legal authorities and functional areas of responsibility and use a collaborative process to establish, identify, and rank incident priorities and to determine appropriate objectives consistent with the priorities. Agencies that are involved in the incident but lack jurisdictional responsibility or authorities are defined as supporting and/or assisting agencies. They are represented in the command structure and effect coordination on behalf of their parent agency through the Liaison Officer. Jurisdictional responsibilities of multiple incident management officials are consolidated into a single planning process that includes:

- Responsibilities for incident management.
- Incident objectives.
- Resource availability and capabilities.
- Limitations.
- Areas of agreement and disagreement between agency officials.

Incidents are managed under a single collaborative approach that includes:

- Common organizational structure.
- Single Incident Command Post.
- Unified planning process.
- Unified resource management.

Comparison of Single IC and UC

Single Incident Commander:

The IC is solely responsible (within the confines of his or her authority) for establishing incident objectives and strategies. The IC is directly responsible for ensuring that all functional area activities are directed toward accomplishment of the strategy.

Unified Command:

The individuals designated by their jurisdictional or organizational authorities (or by departments within a single jurisdiction) must jointly determine objectives, strategies, plans, resource allocations, and priorities and work together to execute integrated incident operations and maximize the use of assigned resources.

Under UC, the IAP is assembled by the Planning Section and is approved by the UC. A single individual, the Operations Section Chief, directs the tactical implementation of the IAP. The Operations Section Chief will usually come from the organization with the greatest jurisdictional involvement. UC participants will agree on the designation of the Operations Section Chief.

UC works best when the participating members of the UC co-locate at the ICP and observe the following practices:

- Select an Operations Section Chief for each operational period.
- Keep each other informed of specific requirements.
- Establish consolidated incident objectives, priorities, and strategies.
- Establish a single system for ordering resources.
- Develop a consolidated written or oral IAP to be evaluated and updated at regular intervals.
- Establish procedures for joint decisionmaking and documentation.

b. Command Staff

In an incident command organization, the Command Staff typically includes a Public Information Officer, a Safety Officer, and a Liaison Officer, who report directly to the IC/UC and may have assistants as necessary (see Figure 4). Additional positions may be required, depending on the nature, scope, complexity, and location(s) of the incident(s), or according to specific requirements established by the IC/UC.

(1) Public Information Officer

The Public Information Officer is responsible for interfacing with the public and media and/or with other agencies with incident-related information requirements. The Public Information Officer gathers, verifies, coordinates, and disseminates accurate, accessible, and timely information on the incident's cause, size, and current situation; resources committed; and other matters of general interest for both internal and external audiences. The Public Information Officer may also perform a key public information-monitoring role. Whether the command structure is single or unified, only one Public Information Officer should be designated per incident. Assistants may be assigned from other involved agencies, departments, or organizations. The IC/UC must approve the release of all incident-related information. In large-scale incidents or where multiple command posts are established, the Public Information Officer should participate in or lead the Joint Information Center (JIC) in order to ensure consistency in the provision of information to the public.

(2) Safety Officer

The Safety Officer monitors incident operations and advises the IC/UC on all matters relating to operational safety, including the health and safety of emergency responder personnel. The ultimate responsibility for the safe conduct of incident management operations rests with the IC/UC and supervisors at all levels of incident management. The Safety Officer is, in turn, responsible to the IC/UC for the systems and procedures necessary to ensure ongoing assessment of hazardous environments, including the incident Safety Plan, coordination of multiagency safety efforts, and implementation of measures to promote emergency responder safety as well as the general safety of incident operations. The Safety Officer has immediate authority to stop and/or prevent unsafe acts during incident operations. It is important to note that the agencies, organizations, or jurisdictions that contribute to joint safety management efforts do not lose their individual identities or responsibility for their own programs, policies, and personnel. Rather, each contributes to the overall effort to protect all responder personnel involved in incident operations.

(3) Liaison Officer

The Liaison Officer is Incident Command's point of contact for representatives of other governmental agencies, NGOs, and the private sector (with no jurisdiction or legal authority) to provide input on their agency's policies, resource availability, and other incident-related matters. Under either a single-IC or a UC structure, representatives from assisting or cooperating agencies and organizations coordinate through the Liaison Officer. Agency and organizational representatives assigned to an incident must have the authority to speak for their parent agencies or organizations on all matters, following appropriate consultations with their agency leadership. Assistants and personnel from other agencies or organizations, public or private, involved in incident management activities may be assigned to the Liaison Officer to facilitate coordination.

(4) Additional Command Staff

Additional Command Staff positions may also be necessary, depending on the nature and location(s) of the incident or specific requirements established by Incident Command. For example, a legal counsel might be assigned to the Planning Section as a technical specialist or directly to the Command Staff to advise Incident Command on legal matters, such as emergency proclamations, the legality of evacuation and quarantine orders, and legal rights and restrictions pertaining to media access. Similarly, a medical advisor might be designated to provide advice and recommendations to Incident Command about medical and mental health services, mass casualty, acute care, vector control, epidemiology, or mass prophylaxis considerations, particularly in response to a bioterrorism incident. In addition, a special needs advisor might be designated to provide expertise regarding communication, transportation, supervision, and essential services for diverse populations in the affected area.[23]

Figure 4. Incident Command System: Command Staff and General Staff

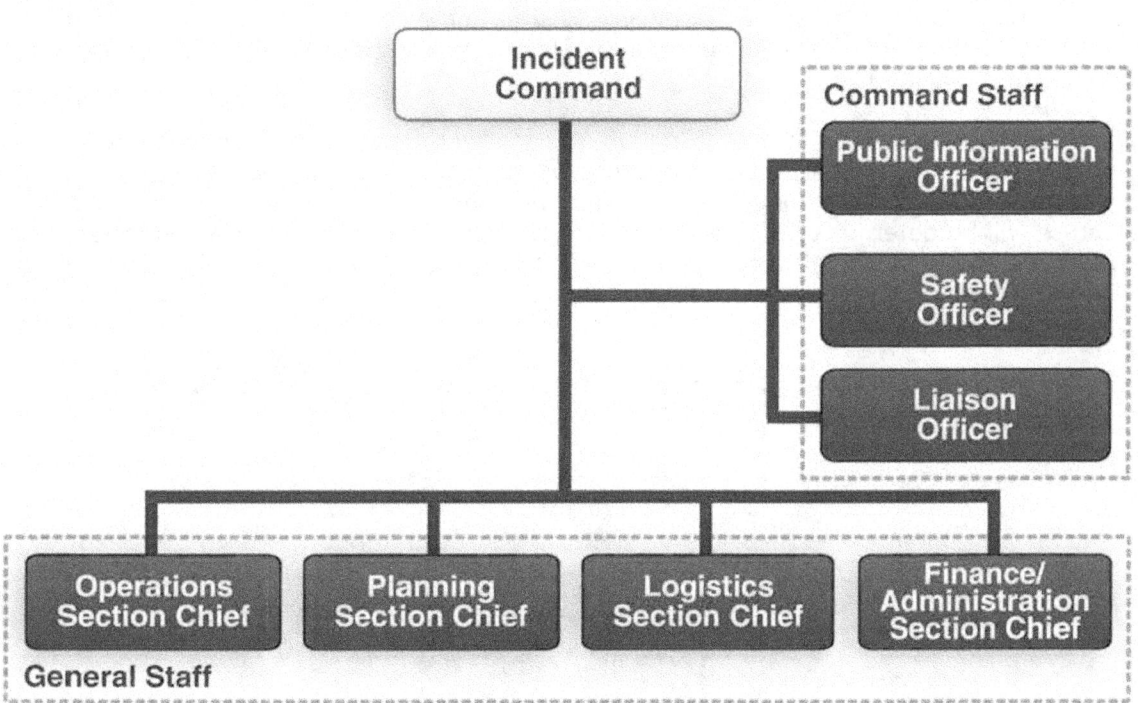

c. Incident Command Organization

The incident Command and Management organization is located at the ICP. Incident Command directs operations from the ICP, which is generally located at or in the immediate vicinity of the incident site. Typically, one ICP is established for each incident. As emergency management/response personnel deploy, they must, regardless of agency affiliation, report to and check in at the designated Staging Area, Base, Camp, or location and notify the IC/UC to receive an assignment in accordance with the procedures established by the IC/UC.

---

[23] See Tab 3, Section F, for more information on technical specialists.

3. GENERAL STAFF

The General Staff is responsible for the functional aspects of the incident command structure. The General Staff typically consists of the Operations, Planning, Logistics, and Finance/Administration Section Chiefs. The Section Chiefs may have one or more deputies assigned, with the assignment of deputies from other agencies encouraged in the case of multijurisdictional incidents. The functional Sections are discussed more fully below.

a. Operations Section

This Section is responsible for all tactical activities focused on reducing the immediate hazard, saving lives and property, establishing situational control, and restoring normal operations. Lifesaving and responder safety will always be the highest priorities and the first objectives in the IAP.

Figure 5 depicts the organizational template for an Operations Section. Expansions of this basic structure may vary according to numerous considerations and operational factors. In some cases, a strictly functional approach may be used. In other cases, the organizational structure will be determined by geographical/jurisdictional boundaries. In still others, a mix of functional and geographical considerations may be appropriate. ICS offers flexibility in determining the right structural approach for the specific circumstances of the incident at hand.

Figure 5. Major Organizational Elements of Operations Section

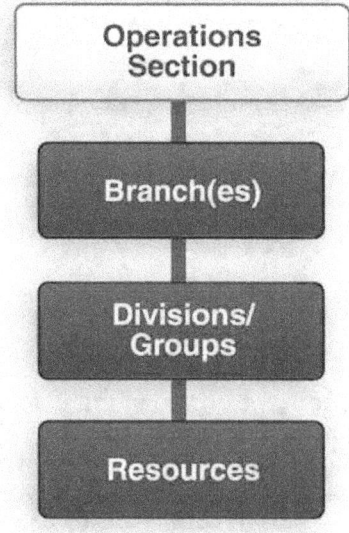

(1) Operations Section Chief

The Operations Section Chief is responsible to Incident Command for the direct management of all incident-related tactical activities. The Operations Section Chief will establish tactics for the assigned operational period. An Operations Section Chief should be designated for each operational period, and responsibilities include direct involvement in development of the IAP.

(2) Branches

Branches may be functional, geographic, or both, depending on the circumstances of the incident. In general, Branches are established when the number of Divisions or Groups exceeds the recommended span of control. Branches are identified by the use of Roman numerals or by functional area.

(3) Divisions and Groups

Divisions and/or Groups are established when the number of resources exceeds the manageable span of control of Incident Command and the Operations Section Chief. Divisions are established to divide an incident into physical or geographical areas of operation. Groups are established to divide the incident into functional areas of operation. For certain types of incidents, for example, Incident Command may assign evacuation or mass-care responsibilities to a functional Group in the Operations Section. Additional levels of supervision may also exist below the Division or Group level.

(4) Resources

Resources may be organized and managed in three different ways, depending on the requirements of the incident.

- **Single Resources:** Individual personnel or equipment and any associated operators.
- **Task Forces:** Any combination of resources assembled in support of a specific mission or operational need. All resource elements within a Task Force must have common communications and a designated leader.
- **Strike Teams:** A set number of resources of the same kind and type that have an established minimum number of personnel. All resource elements within a Strike Team must have common communications and a designated leader.

The use of Task Forces and Strike Teams is encouraged, when appropriate, to optimize the use of resources, reduce the span of control over a large number of single resources, and reduce the complexity of incident management coordination and communications.

b. Planning Section

The Planning Section collects, evaluates, and disseminates incident situation information and intelligence to the IC/UC and incident management personnel. This Section then prepares status reports, displays situation information, maintains the status of resources assigned to the incident, and prepares and documents the IAP, based on Operations Section input and guidance from the IC/UC.

As shown in Figure 6, the Planning Section is comprised of four primary Units, as well as a number of technical specialists to assist in evaluating the situation, developing planning options, and forecasting requirements for additional resources. Within the Planning Section, the following primary Units fulfill functional requirements:

- **Resources Unit:** Responsible for recording the status of resources committed to the incident. This Unit also evaluates resources committed currently to the incident, the effects additional responding resources will have on the incident, and anticipated resource needs.
- **Situation Unit:** Responsible for the collection, organization, and analysis of incident status information, and for analysis of the situation as it progresses.
- **Demobilization Unit:** Responsible for ensuring orderly, safe, and efficient demobilization of incident resources.
- **Documentation Unit:** Responsible for collecting, recording, and safeguarding all documents relevant to the incident.
- **Technical Specialist(s):** Personnel with special skills that can be used anywhere within the ICS organization.

Figure 6. Planning Section Organization

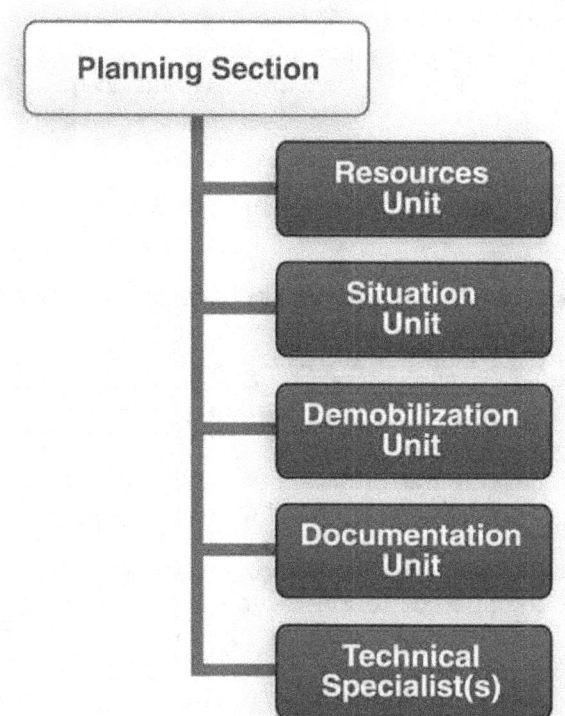

The Planning Section is normally responsible for gathering and disseminating information and intelligence critical to the incident, unless the IC/UC places this function elsewhere. The Planning Section is also responsible for assembling the IAP. The IAP includes the overall incident objectives and strategies established by Incident Command. In the case of a UC, the IAP must adequately address the mission and policy needs of each jurisdictional agency, as well as interaction between jurisdictions, functional agencies, and private organizations. The IAP also addresses tactics and support activities required for the planned operational period, generally 12 to 24 hours.

The IAP should incorporate changes in strategies and tactics based on lessons learned during earlier operational periods. A written IAP is especially important when:

- Resources from multiple agencies and/or jurisdictions are involved;
- The incident will span several operational periods;
- Changes in shifts of personnel and/or equipment are required; or
- There is a need to document actions and decisions.

The IAP will typically contain a number of components, as shown in Table 5.

Table 5. Sample IAP Outline

Component	Normally Prepared By
Incident Objectives (Form: ICS 202)	Incident Commander
Organization Assignment List or Chart (Form: ICS 203)	Resources Unit
Assignment List (Form: ICS 204)	Resources Unit
Incident Radio Communications Plan (Form: ICS 205)	Communications Unit
Medical Plan (Form: ICS 206)	Medical Unit
Incident Maps	Situation Unit
General Safety Message/Site Safety Plan	Safety Officer
Other Potential Components (Incident dependent)	
Air Operations Summary	Air Operations
Traffic Plan	Ground Support Unit
Decontamination Plan	Technical Specialist
Waste Management or Disposal Plan	Technical Specialist
Demobilization Plan	Demobilization Unit
Site Security Plan	Law Enforcement, Technical Specialist, or Security Manager
Investigative Plan	Law Enforcement
Evidence Recovery Plan	Law Enforcement
Evacuation Plan	As required
Sheltering/Mass Care Plan	As required
Other (as required)	As required

c. Logistics Section

The Logistics Section (see Figure 7) is responsible for all service support requirements needed to facilitate effective and efficient incident management, including ordering resources from off-incident locations. This Section also provides facilities, security (of the incident command facilities and personnel), transportation, supplies, equipment maintenance and fuel, food services, communications and information technology support, and emergency responder medical services, including inoculations, as required. Within the Logistics Section, six primary Units fulfill functional requirements:

- **Supply Unit:** Orders, receives, stores, and processes all incident-related resources, personnel, and supplies.
- **Ground Support Unit:** Provides all ground transportation during an incident. In conjunction with providing transportation, the Unit is also responsible for maintaining and supplying vehicles, keeping usage records, and developing incident Traffic Plans.
- **Facilities Unit:** Sets up, maintains, and demobilizes all facilities used in support of incident operations. The Unit also provides facility maintenance and security services required to support incident operations.
- **Food Unit:** Determines food and water requirements, plans menus, orders food, provides cooking facilities, cooks, serves, maintains food service areas, and manages food security and safety concerns.
- **Communications Unit:** Major responsibilities include effective communications planning as well as acquiring, setting up, maintaining, and accounting for communications equipment.
- **Medical Unit:** Responsible for the effective and efficient provision of medical services to incident personnel.

Figure 7. Logistics Section Organization

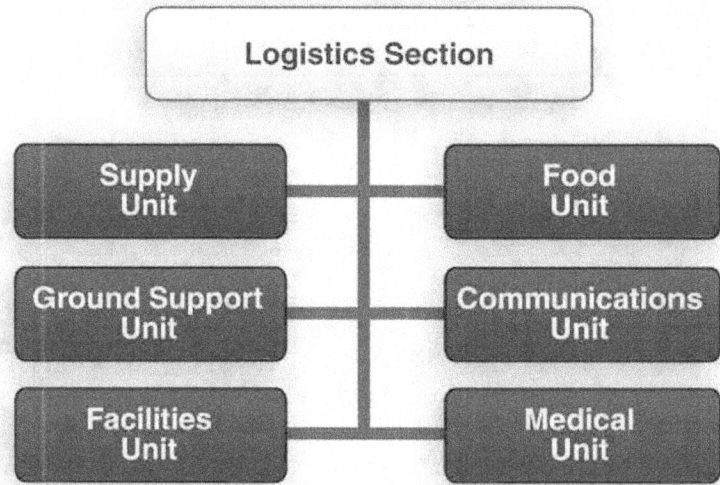

d. Finance/Administration Section

A Finance/Administration Section is established when the incident management activities require on-scene or incident-specific finance and other administrative support services. Some of the functions that fall within the scope of this Section are recording personnel time, maintaining vendor contracts, administering compensation and claims, and conducting an overall cost analysis for the incident. If a separate Section is established, close coordination with the Planning Section and Logistics Section is also essential so that operational records can be reconciled with financial documents.

The Finance/Administration Section is a critical part of ICS in large, complex incidents involving significant funding originating from multiple sources. In addition to monitoring multiple sources of funds, the Section Chief must track and report to Incident Command the accrued cost as the incident progresses. This allows the IC/UC to forecast the need for additional funds before operations are negatively affected. Figure 8 illustrates the basic organizational structure for a Finance/Administration Section. When such a Section is established, the depicted Units may be staffed as required. Within the Finance/Administration Section, four primary Units fulfill functional requirements:

- **Compensation/Claims Unit:** Responsible for financial concerns resulting from property damage, injuries, or fatalities at the incident.
- **Cost Unit:** Responsible for tracking costs, analyzing cost data, making estimates, and recommending cost savings measures.
- **Procurement Unit:** Responsible for financial matters concerning vendor contracts.
- **Time Unit:** Responsible for recording time for incident personnel and hired equipment.

Figure 8. Finance/Administration Section Organization

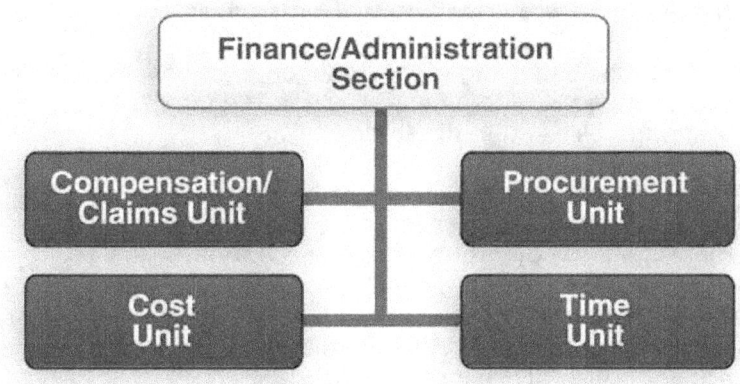

e. Intelligence/Investigations Function

The collection, analysis, and sharing of incident-related intelligence are important elements of ICS. Normally, operational information and situational intelligence are management functions located in the Planning Section, with a focus on three incident intelligence areas: situation status, resource status, and anticipated incident status or escalation (e.g., weather forecasts and location of supplies). This information and intelligence is utilized for incident management decisionmaking. In addition, technical specialists in the Planning Section may be utilized to provide specific information that supports tactical decisions.

Incident management organizations must also establish a system for the collection, analysis, and sharing of information developed during intelligence/investigation efforts. Some incidents require intelligence and investigative information, which is defined in either of two ways. First, it is defined as information that leads to the detection, prevention, apprehension, and prosecution of criminal activities or the individuals involved, including terrorist incidents. Second, it is defined as information that leads to determination of the cause, projection of spread, assessment of impact, or selection of countermeasures for a given incident (regardless of the source) such as public health events, disease outbreaks, or fires with unknown origins.

ICS allows for organizational flexibility, so the Intelligence/Investigations Function can be embedded in several different places within the organizational structure.

- **Within the Planning Section:** This is the traditional placement for this function and is appropriate for incidents with little or no investigative information requirements nor a significant amount of specialized information.
- **As a Separate General Staff Section:** This option may be appropriate when a there is a significant intelligence/investigations component to the incident for criminal or epidemiological purposes or when multiple investigative agencies are involved. A separate Intelligence/Investigations Section may be needed when highly specialized information requiring technical analysis is both critical and time sensitive to lifesaving operations (e.g., chemical, biological, radiological, or nuclear incidents) or when there is a need for classified intelligence.
- **Within the Operations Section:** This option may be appropriate for incidents that require a high degree of linkage and coordination between the investigative information and the operational tactics that are being employed.
- **Within the Command Staff:** This option may be appropriate for incidents with little need for tactical information or classified intelligence and where supporting Agency Representatives are providing real-time information to the IC/UC.

The mission of the Intelligence/Investigations Function is to ensure that all investigative and intelligence operations, functions, and activities within the incident response are properly managed, coordinated, and directed in order to:

- Prevent/deter additional activity, incidents, or attacks.
- Collect, process, analyze, and appropriately disseminate intelligence information.
- Conduct a thorough and comprehensive investigation.
- Identify, process, collect, create a chain of custody for, safeguard, examine/analyze, and store all probative evidence.
- Determine source or cause and control spread and impact, in the investigation of emerging incidents (fire, disease outbreak, etc.).

The Intelligence/Investigations Function has responsibilities that cross all interests of departments involved during an incident; however, certain functions remain specific to law enforcement response and mission areas. Two examples of these are to expeditiously identify and apprehend all perpetrators, and to successfully prosecute all defendants.

Regardless of how the Intelligence/Investigations Function is organized, a close liaison will be maintained, and information will be transmitted to Incident Command, the Operations Section, and the Planning Section. However, classified information requiring a security clearance, sensitive information, or specific investigative tactics that would compromise the investigation will be shared only with those who have the appropriate security clearance or a need to know.

The Intelligence/Investigations Function can be organized in a variety of ways. The following are examples of Groups that may be activated if needed:

- **Investigative Operations Group:** Responsible for overall investigative effort.
- **Intelligence Group:** Responsible for obtaining unclassified, classified, and open source intelligence.
- **Forensic Group:** Responsible for collection and integrity of forensic evidence, and in incidents of a criminal nature, the integrity of the crime scene.
- **Investigative Support Group:** Responsible for ensuring that required investigative personnel are made available expeditiously and that the necessary resources are properly distributed, maintained, safeguarded, stored, and returned, when appropriate.

Other Groups may be created to handle the following responsibilities: ensuring that missing or unidentified persons and human remains are investigated and identified expeditiously and that required notifications are made in a timely manner. These responsibilities include the collection of ante mortem information and exemplars in a family assistance center.

4. INCIDENT MANAGEMENT TEAMS

An IMT is an incident command organization made up of the Command and General Staff members and other appropriate personnel in an ICS organization and can be deployed or activated, as needed. National, State, and some local IMTs have formal certification and qualification, notification, deployment, and operational procedures in place. In other cases, IMTs are formed at an incident or for specific events. The level of training and experience of the IMT members, coupled with the IMT's identified formal response requirements and responsibilities, are factors in determining an IMT's type, or level.

5. INCIDENT COMPLEX: MULTIPLE INCIDENT MANAGEMENT WITHIN A SINGLE ICS ORGANIZATION

a. Description

An Incident Complex refers to two or more individual incidents located in the same general area that are assigned to a single IC or a UC. When an Incident Complex is established over several individual incidents, the general guideline is that the previously identified incidents become Branches within the Operations Section of the IMT. This provides greater potential for future expansion if required. Each Branch thus has the increased flexibility to establish Divisions or Groups. Additionally, because Divisions and Groups may already have been established at each of the incidents, the same basic structure can be propagated. If any of the incidents within a complex has the potential to become a large-scale incident, it is best to establish it as a separate incident with its own ICS organization.

The following are examples where a complex may be appropriate:

- An earthquake, tornado, flood, or other situation where many separate incidents are occurring in close proximity.
- Several similar incidents are occurring in close proximity to one another.
- One incident underway with an IMT assigned, with other smaller incidents occurring in the same area.

A complex may be managed under a single IC or a UC. The following are additional considerations for the use of a complex:

- The incidents are close enough to be managed by the same IMT.
- A combined management approach could achieve some staff or logistical support economies.
- The number of overall incidents within the jurisdiction requires consolidations wherever possible to conserve staff and reduce costs.
- A single Incident Command can adequately provide Planning, Logistics, and Finance/Administration activities to the complex.

6. AREA COMMAND

a. Description

Area Command is an organization to oversee the management of multiple incidents handled individually by separate ICS organizations or to oversee the management of a very large or evolving incident engaging multiple IMTs. An Agency Administrator/Executive or other public official with jurisdictional responsibility for the incident usually makes the decision to establish an Area Command. An Area Command is activated only if necessary, depending on the complexity of the incident and incident management span-of-control considerations.

Area Commands are particularly relevant to incidents that are typically not site specific, are not immediately identifiable, are geographically dispersed, and evolve over longer periods of time (e.g., public health emergencies, earthquakes, tornadoes, civil disturbances, and any geographic area where several IMTs are being used and these incidents are all requesting similar resources). Incidents such as these, as well as acts of biological, chemical, radiological, and nuclear terrorism, require a coordinated intergovernmental, NGO, and private-sector response, with large-scale coordination typically conducted at a higher jurisdictional level. Area Command is also used when a number of incidents of the same type in the same area are competing for the same resources, such as multiple hazardous material incidents, spills, or fires.

When incidents are of different types and/or do not have similar resource demands, they are usually handled as separate incidents or are coordinated through an Emergency Operations Center (EOC) or Multiagency Coordination Group (MAC Group). If the incidents under the authority of the Area Command span multiple jurisdictions, a Unified Area Command should be established (see Figure 9). This allows each jurisdiction to have appropriate representation in the Area Command.

Area Command should not be confused with the functions performed by MACS: Area Command oversees management coordination of the incident(s), while a MACS element, such as a communications/dispatch center, EOC, or MAC Group, coordinates support.

Figure 9. Chain of Command and Reporting Relationships

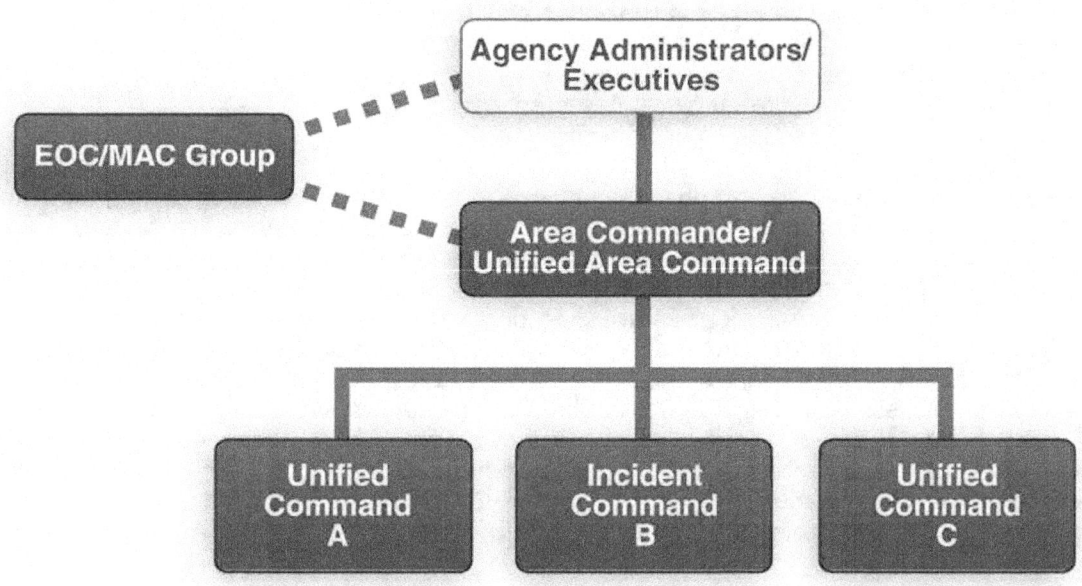

The dotted line connecting EOC/MAC Group with the Agency Administrators/Executives and Area Commander/Unified Area Command represents the coordination and communication link between an EOC/MAC Group and the Command structure.

b. Responsibilities

For incidents under its authority, an Area Command has the following responsibilities:

- Develop broad objectives for the impacted area(s).
- Coordinate the development of individual incident objectives and strategies.
- (Re)allocate resources as the established priorities change.
- Ensure that incidents are properly managed.
- Ensure effective communications.
- Ensure that incident management objectives are met and do not conflict with each other or with agency policies.
- Identify critical resource needs and report them to the established EOC/MAC Groups.
- Ensure that short-term "emergency" recovery is coordinated to assist in the transition to full recovery operations.

B. Multiagency Coordination Systems

Multiagency coordination is a <u>process</u> that allows all levels of government and all disciplines to work together more efficiently and effectively. Multiagency coordination occurs across the different disciplines involved in incident management, across jurisdictional lines, or across levels of government.

> MACS is a system . . .
> not simply a facility.

Multiagency coordination can and does occur on a regular basis whenever personnel from different agencies interact in such activities as preparedness, prevention, response, recovery, and mitigation. Often, cooperating agencies develop a MACS to better define how they will work together and to work together more efficiently; however, multiagency coordination can take place without established protocols. MACS may be put in motion regardless of the location, personnel titles, or organizational structure. MACS includes planning and coordinating resources and other support for planned, notice, or no-notice events. MACS defines business practices, standard operating procedures, processes, and protocols by which participating agencies will coordinate their interactions. Integral elements of MACS are dispatch procedures and protocols, the incident command structure, and the coordination and support activities taking place within an activated EOC. Fundamentally, MACS provide support, coordination, and assistance with policy-level decisions to the ICS structure managing an incident.

Written agreements allow agencies within the system to conduct activities using established rules and are often self-defined by the participating organizations. A fully implemented MACS is critical for seamless multiagency coordination activities and essential to the success and safety of the response whenever more than one jurisdictional agency responds. Moreover, the use of MACS is one of the fundamental components of Command and Management within NIMS, as it promotes scalability and flexibility necessary for a coordinated response.

1. DEFINITION

The primary function of MACS is to coordinate activities above the field level and to prioritize the incident demands for critical or competing resources, thereby assisting the coordination of the operations in the field. MACS consists of a combination of elements: personnel, procedures, protocols, business practices, and communications integrated into a common system. For the purpose of coordinating resources and support between multiple jurisdictions, MACS can be implemented from a fixed facility or by other arrangements outlined within the system.

In some instances, MACS is informal and based on oral agreements between jurisdictions, but usually it is more formalized and supported by written agreements, operational procedures, and protocols. The formal process, where issues are addressed before an incident occurs, is the preferred and recommended approach, as it streamlines the coordination function. While ad hoc arrangements between jurisdictions may result in effective multiagency coordination on relatively minor incidents, coordination on larger, more complex incidents is most successful when it takes place within a planned and well-established system.

Figure 10 illustrates an overview of MACS as it transitions over the course of an incident. The graphic shows how an incident begins, with the on-scene single command; as it grows in size and complexity, potentially developing into a Unified Command, the incident may require off-scene coordination and support.

2. SYSTEM ELEMENTS

MACS includes a combination of facilities, equipment, personnel, and procedures integrated into a common system with responsibility for coordination of resources and support to emergency operations.

Figure 10. Multiagency Coordination System (MACS)

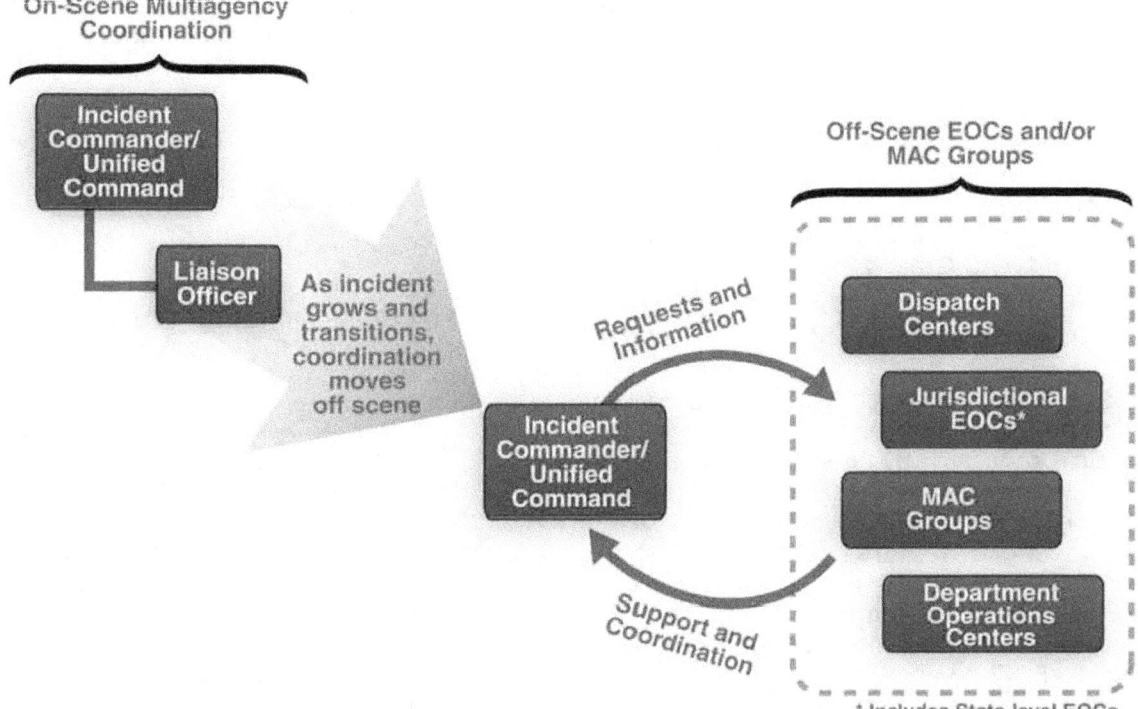

a. Facilities

The need for location(s)—such as a communications/dispatch center, EOC, city hall, virtual location—to house system activities will depend on the anticipated functions of the system.

b. Equipment

To accomplish system activities, equipment (such as computers and phones) must be identified and procured.

c. Personnel

Typical personnel include Agency Administrators/Executives, or their appointed representatives, who are authorized to commit agency resources and funds in a coordinated response effort. Personnel can also be authorized representatives from supporting agencies, NGOs, and the private sector who assist in coordinating activities above the field level.

d. Procedures

Procedures include processes, protocols, agreements, and business practices that prescribe the activities, relationships, and functionality of the MACS. Identifying the interactive communications activities and associated implementation plans are critical components of the system.

3. EXAMPLES OF SYSTEM ELEMENTS

The two most commonly used elements of the Multiagency Coordination System are EOCs and MAC Groups.

a. Emergency Operations Center

EOCs may be organized by major discipline (e.g., fire, law enforcement, or emergency medical services); by emergency support function (e.g., transportation, communications, public works and engineering, or resource support); by jurisdiction (e.g., city, county, or region); or, more likely, by some combination thereof. ICPs need good communication links to EOCs to ensure effective and efficient incident management.

Often, agencies within a political jurisdiction will establish coordination, communications, control, logistics, etc., at the department level for conducting overall management of their assigned resources. Governmental departments (or agencies, bureaus, etc.) or private organizations may also have operations centers (referred to here as Department Operations Centers, or DOCs) that serve as the interface between the ongoing operations of that organization and the emergency operations it is supporting. The DOC may directly support the incident and receive information relative to its operations. In most cases, DOCs are

An EOC is activated:

- To support the on-scene response during an escalating incident by relieving the burden of external coordination and securing additional resources.

An EOC is:

- A physical location.
- Staffed with personnel trained for and authorized to represent their agency/discipline.
- Equipped with mechanisms for communicating with the incident site and obtaining resources and potential resources.
- Managed through protocols.
- Applicable at different levels of government.

An EOC consists of:

- Personnel and equipment appropriate to the level of incident.

An EOC is used:

- In varying ways within all levels of government and the private sector.
- To provide coordination, direction, and support during emergencies.

An EOC may:

- Facilitate MACS functions and may be needed to support Area Command, IC, or UC when resource needs exceed local capabilities.

An EOC does not:

- Command the on-scene level of the incident.

physically represented in a combined agency EOC by authorized agent(s) for the department or agency.

EOCs may be staffed by personnel representing multiple jurisdictions and functional disciplines and a wide variety of resources. For example, a local EOC established in response to a bioterrorism incident would likely include a mix of law enforcement, emergency management, public health, and medical personnel (local, State, or Federal public health officials and possibly representatives of health care facilities, emergency medical services, etc.).

The physical size, staffing, and equipping of an EOC will depend on the size of the jurisdiction, resources available, and anticipated incident management workload. EOCs may be organized and staffed in a variety of ways. Regardless of its specific organizational structure, an EOC should include the following core functions: coordination; communications; resource allocation and tracking; and information collection, analysis, and dissemination.

Upon activation of a local EOC, communications and coordination must be established between Incident Command and the EOC. ICS field organizations must also establish communications with the activated local EOC, either directly or through their parent organizations. Additionally, EOCs at all levels of government and across functional agencies must be capable of communicating appropriately with other EOCs, including those maintained by private organizations. Communications between EOCs must be reliable and contain built-in redundancies. The efficient functioning of EOCs most frequently depends on the existence of mutual aid agreements and joint communications protocols among participating agencies.

b. MAC Group

Typically, Agency Administrators/Executives, or their designees, who are authorized to represent or commit agency resources and funds are brought together to form MAC Groups. MAC Groups may also be known as multiagency committees, emergency management committees, or as otherwise defined by the system. Personnel assigned to the EOC who meet the criteria for participation in a MAC Group may be asked to fulfill that role.

A MAC Group does not have any direct incident involvement and will often be located some distance from the incident site(s). In many cases a MAC Group can function virtually to accomplish its assigned tasks.

A MAC Group may require a support organization for its own logistics and documentation needs; to manage incident-related decision support information such as tracking critical resources, situation status, and intelligence or investigative information; and to provide public information to the news media and public. The number and skills of its personnel will vary by incident complexity, activity levels, needs of the MAC Group, and other factors identified through agreements or by preparedness organizations. A MAC Group may be established at any level (e.g., national, State, or local) or within any discipline (e.g., emergency management, public health, critical infrastructure, or private sector).

4. PRIMARY FUNCTIONS OF MACS

The Multiagency Coordination System should be both flexible and scalable to be efficient and effective. MACS will generally perform common functions during an incident; however, not all of the system's functions will be performed during every incident, and functions may not occur in any particular order.

a. Situation Assessment

This assessment includes the collection, processing, and display of all information needed. This may take the form of consolidating situation reports, obtaining supplemental information, and preparing maps and status boards.

b. Incident Priority Determination

Establishing the priorities among ongoing incidents within the defined area of responsibility is another component of MACS. Typically, a process or procedure is established to coordinate with Area or Incident Commands to prioritize the incident demands for critical resources. Additional considerations for determining priorities include the following:

- Life-threatening situations.
- Threat to property.
- High damage potential.
- Incident complexity.
- Environmental impact.
- Economic impact.
- Other criteria established by the Multiagency Coordination System.

c. Critical Resource Acquisition and Allocation

Designated critical resources will be acquired, if possible, from the involved agencies or jurisdictions. These agencies or jurisdictions may shift resources internally to match the incident needs as a result of incident priority decisions. Resources available from incidents in the process of demobilization may be shifted, for example, to higher priority incidents.

Resources may also be acquired from outside the affected area. Procedures for acquiring outside resources will vary, depending on such things as the agencies involved and written agreements.

d. Support for Relevant Incident Management Policies and Interagency Activities

A primary function of MACS is to coordinate, support, and assist with policy-level decisions and interagency activities relevant to incident management activities, policies, priorities, and strategies.

e. Coordination With Other MACS Elements

A critical part of MACS is outlining how each system element will communicate and coordinate with other system elements at the same level, the level above, and the level below. Those involved in multiagency coordination functions following an incident may be responsible for incorporating lessons learned into their procedures, protocols, business practices, and communications strategies. These improvements may need to be coordinated with other appropriate preparedness organizations.

f. Coordination With Elected and Appointed Officials

Another primary function outlined in MACS is a process or procedure to keep elected and appointed officials at all levels of government informed. Maintaining the awareness and support of these officials, particularly those from jurisdictions within the affected area, is extremely important, as scarce resources may need to move to an agency or jurisdiction with higher priorities.

g. Coordination of Summary Information

By virtue of the situation assessment function, personnel implementing the multiagency coordination procedures may provide summary information on incidents within their area of responsibility as well as provide agency/jurisdictional contacts for media and other interested agencies.

5. DIFFERENCES BETWEEN A MAC GROUP AND AREA COMMAND

MAC Groups are often confused with Area Command (as defined earlier in Component IV). Table 6 highlights some of the primary differences between the two.

Table 6. Differences Between a MAC Group and Area Command

MAC Group	Area Command
Off-scene coordination and support organization with no direct incident authority or responsibility.	Management function of ICS with oversight responsibility and authority of IMTs assigned at multiple incidents. Area Command may be established as Unified Area Command.
Members are Agency Administrators/ Executives or designees from the agencies involved or heavily committed to the incident.	Members are the most highly skilled incident management personnel.
Organization generally consists of multiagency coordination personnel (including Agency Administrators/Executives), MAC Group coordinator, and an intelligence and information support staff.	Organization generally consists of an Area Commander, Assistant Area Commander—Planning, and Assistant Area Commander—Logistics.
Members are Agency Administrators/ Executives or designees.	Authority for specific incident(s) is delegated from the Agency Administrator/Executive.
Allocates and reallocates critical resources through the communications/dispatch system by setting incident priorities.	Assigns and reassigns critical resources allocated to it by MACS or the normal communications/dispatch system organization.
Makes coordinated decisions at the Agency Administrator/Executive level on issues that affect multiple agencies.	Ensures that incident objectives and strategies are complementary between IMTs.

C. PUBLIC INFORMATION

1. INTRODUCTION

Public Information consists of the processes, procedures, and systems to communicate timely, accurate, and accessible information on the incident's cause, size, and current situation to the public, responders, and additional stakeholders (both directly affected and indirectly affected). Public information must be coordinated and integrated across jurisdictions, agencies, and organizations; among Federal, State, tribal, and local governments; and with NGOs and the private sector. Well-developed public information, education strategies, and communications plans help to ensure that lifesaving measures, evacuation routes, threat and alert systems, and other public safety information are coordinated and communicated to numerous audiences in a timely, consistent manner.

2. SYSTEM DESCRIPTION AND COMPONENTS

a. Public Information Officer

The Public Information Officer supports the incident command structure as a member of the Command staff. The Public Information Officer advises the IC/UC on all public information matters relating to the management of the incident. The Public Information Officer also handles inquiries from the media, the public, and elected officials; emergency public information and warnings; rumor monitoring and response; media relations; and other functions required to gather, verify, coordinate, and disseminate accurate, accessible, and timely information related to the incident. Information on public health, safety, and protection is of particular importance. Public Information Officers are able to create coordinated and consistent messages by collaborating to:

> **Roles of Public Information Officer**
>
> **The Public Information Officer gathers, verifies, coordinates, and disseminates accurate, accessible, and timely information on the incident's cause, size, and current situation; resources committed; and other matters of general interest for both internal and external use.**

- Identify key information that needs to be communicated to the public.
- Craft messages conveying key information that are clear and easily understood by all, including those with special needs.
- Prioritize messages to ensure timely delivery of information without overwhelming the audience.
- Verify accuracy of information through appropriate channels.
- Disseminate messages using the most effective means available.

b. Joint Information System

The Joint Information System (JIS) provides the mechanism to organize, integrate, and coordinate information to ensure timely, accurate, accessible, and consistent messaging across multiple jurisdictions and/or disciplines with NGOs and the private sector. The JIS includes the plans, protocols, procedures, and structures used to provide public information. Federal, State, tribal, territorial, regional, or local Public Information Officers and established JICs are critical supporting elements of the JIS. Key elements include the following:

- Interagency coordination and integration.
- Gathering, verifying, coordinating, and disseminating consistent messages.
- Support for decisionmakers.
- Flexibility, modularity, and adaptability.

c. Joint Information Center

The JIC is a central location that facilitates operation of the JIS, where personnel with public information responsibilities perform critical emergency information functions, crisis communications, and public affairs functions. JICs may be established at various levels of government or at incident sites, or can be components of Federal, State, tribal, territorial, regional, or local MACS (e.g., MAC Groups or EOCs). Depending on the requirements of the incident, an incident-specific JIC is typically established at a single, on-scene location in coordination with Federal, State, and local agencies, or at the national level if the situation warrants. Releases are cleared through the IC/UC, EOC/MAC Group, and/or Federal officials in the case of federally coordinated incidents to

> **Possibility of a Virtual JIC**
>
> A JIC may involve real-time, constant links to other sites, thus creating a virtual JIC. All participants should be fully integrated and linked into the JIC so that it functions as a single-site operation.
>
> Advantages include:
> - Rapid establishment of the JIC functions.
> - Access to expanded resources.
> - Relationship building.

ensure consistent messages, avoid release of conflicting information, and prevent negative impact on operations. This formal process for releasing information ensures the protection of incident-sensitive information. Agencies may issue their own releases related to their policies, procedures, programs, and capabilities; however, these should be coordinated with the incident-specific JIC(s).

A single JIC location is preferable, but the system is flexible and adaptable enough to accommodate multiple physical or virtual JIC locations. For example, multiple JICs may be needed for a complex incident spanning a wide geographic area or multiple jurisdictions. In instances when multiple JICs are activated, information must be coordinated among all appropriate JICs; each JIC must have procedures and protocols to communicate and coordinate effectively with one another. Whenever there are multiple JICs, the final release authority must be the senior command, whether using Unified or Area Command structures. A national JIC may be used when an incident requires Federal coordination and is expected to be of long duration (e.g., weeks or months) or when the incident affects a large area of the country.

In light of the need for real-time communications, JICs can be organized in many ways, depending on the nature of the incident.

Table 7 identifies several types of JICs.

Table 7. Types of Joint Information Centers

Incident	• Optimal physical location for local and IC-assigned Public Information Officers to co-locate • Easy media access is paramount to success
Virtual	• Established when physical co-location is not feasible • Incorporates technology and communication protocols
Satellite	• Smaller in scale than other JICs • Established primarily to support the incident JIC • Operates under the control of the primary JIC for that incident • Is not independent of that direction
Area	• Supports wide-area multiple-incident ICS structures • Could be established on a local or statewide basis • Media access is paramount
Support	• Established to support several incident JICs in multiple States • Offers supplemental staff and resources outside of the disaster area
National	• Established for long-duration incidents • Established to support Federal response activities • Staffed by numerous Federal departments and/or agencies • Media access is paramount

d. Organizational Independence

Organizations participating in incident management retain their independence. Incident Command and MACS are responsible for establishing and overseeing JICs, including processes for coordinating and clearing public communications. In the case of Unified Command, the departments, agencies, organizations, or jurisdictions that contribute to joint public information management do not lose their individual identities or responsibility for their own programs or policies. Rather, each agency/organization contributes to the overall unified message.

e. Getting Information to the Public and Additional Stakeholders

The process of getting information to the public and additional stakeholders during an incident is an ongoing cycle that involves four steps.

(1) Gathering Information

Gathering information is the first step in the process of getting information to the public and additional stakeholders. Information is collected from:

- **On-Scene Command:** A source of ongoing, official information on the response effort.
- **On-Scene Public Information Officers:** Report to the JIC what they are observing and hearing at the incident from the news media, elected officials and their staff, and the public.

- **Media Monitoring:** Used to assess the accuracy and content of news media reports. It also helps to identify trends and breaking issues.
- **News Media:** A valuable source of developing information and current issues.
- **Public and Elected/Appointed Officials:** Inquiries from elected/appointed officials, community leaders, and the general public point to the specific concerns of those in the affected areas.

(2) Verifying Information

The next step in the process is to verify the accuracy of the information that has been collected, by consulting the following sources:

- **Other Public Information Officers in the JIC:** Comparing notes—especially with the lead Public Information Officer and Public Information Officers who are liaisons to the various assistance programs or response/recovery partners—is one way to verify information accuracy.
- **EOC Sources:** Including program leads, who should be asked to confirm information.
- **On-Scene Public Information Officers:** A valuable source for checking the accuracy of information reported to the EOC with reports from the news media, the offices of elected officials, and people on the scene.

(3) Coordinating Information

The next step in the process is to coordinate with other Public Information Officers who are part of the JIS. These Public Information Officers include both those represented in the JIC and those working from another location who are part of the JIS. Coordinating information involves:

- **Establishing Key Message(s):** After gathering information from all sources, unified messages are crafted that address all informational needs and are prioritized according to the overall Federal, State, tribal, and local response/recovery strategy. The mission includes getting accurate, consistent information to the right people at the right time so they can make informed decisions.
- **Obtaining Approval/Clearance From Those With Authority:** Ensuring that the information is consistent, accurate, and accessible. The approval process should be streamlined, however, to ensure that the information is released in a timely manner.

(4) Disseminating Information

The next step in the process is to disseminate information to the public and additional stakeholders. This step involves:

- **Using Multiple Methods:** In an emergency, there may not be many options. Phone calls and interviews might be the primary means of getting information to the news media. Personal visits or town meetings may be the most effective avenue for the public, elected/appointed officials, or other stakeholders. These outreach efforts can be supported by providing talking points and fliers to on-scene Public Information Officers.
- **Monitoring the Media:** Media monitoring is invaluable for ensuring that the message is understood by the news media and reported accurately and completely. Important inaccuracies should be addressed before they are reported incorrectly a second time.

3. PUBLIC INFORMATION COMMUNICATIONS PLANNING

Information communications strategies and planning are essential to all aspects of public information. Plans should include processes, protocols, and procedures that require the development of draft news releases; media lists; and contact information for elected/appointed officials, community leaders, private-sector organizations, and public service organizations to facilitate the dissemination of accurate, consistent, accessible, and timely public information. Public information communications should be a critical component of training and exercises.

D. RELATIONSHIPS AMONG COMMAND AND MANAGEMENT ELEMENTS

ICS, MACS, and Public Information have been described herein as separate elements of Command and Management within NIMS. However, NIMS relies on the relationships among these elements along with the elements themselves.

Some relationships are specifically defined. For example, an Area Command or Incident Command coordinates with Public Information on incident-specific public information through an incident Public Information Officer within the JIS. The relationship between Area Command or Incident Command and MACS is primarily defined by a communications link between Command and/or field-level personnel with resource management responsibilities and a particular staff position within multiagency coordination.

These relationships—along with other relationships among Command and Management elements that are not as clearly defined in advance—must be clearly defined and documented as each element evolves during an incident.

COMPONENT V: ONGOING MANAGEMENT AND MAINTENANCE

The Ongoing Management and Maintenance component of NIMS contains two subsections: the National Integration Center (NIC) and Supporting Technologies. The NIC section of the document sets forth the responsibilities of the NIC. The Supporting Technologies Section discusses principles necessary to leverage science and technology to improve capabilities and lower costs.

A. NATIONAL INTEGRATION CENTER

Homeland Security Presidential Directive 5 required the Secretary of Homeland Security to establish a mechanism for ensuring the ongoing management and maintenance of NIMS, including regular consultation with other Federal departments and agencies; State, tribal, and local stakeholders; nongovernmental organizations (NGOs); and the private sector. To this end, the Secretary established the NIC to serve as an informational assistance resource for government agencies at all levels, NGOs, and the private sector that are implementing NIMS. The NIC provides strategic direction for and oversight of NIMS, supporting routine maintenance and continuous refinement of the system and its components over the long term. The NIC solicits participation from Federal departments and agencies; State, tribal, and local governments; and emergency management/response personnel,[24] including those from NGOs and the private sector. Revisions to NIMS and other issues can be proposed by all NIMS users (including Federal, State, tribal, substate regional, and local governments, as well as the private sector, voluntary organizations, academia, nonprofit organizations, and other NIMS-related professional associations).

Additionally, the NIC administers NIMS compliance requirements, facilitates the development of guidance standards for typing and credentialing, supports NIMS training and exercises, and manages the publication of various NIMS-related materials.

1. CONCEPTS AND PRINCIPLES

The process for managing and maintaining NIMS ensures that all users and stakeholders—including all levels of government, functional disciplines, NGOs, and the private sector—are given the opportunity to participate in NIC activities. The NIMS management and maintenance process relies heavily on lessons learned from actual incidents and incident management training and exercises, as well as recognized best practices across jurisdictions and functional disciplines.

---

[24] Emergency management/response personnel include Federal, State, territorial, tribal, substate regional, and local governments, nongovernmental organizations, private-sector organizations, critical infrastructure owners and operators, and all other organizations and individuals who assume an emergency management role.

2. NIMS REVISION PROCESS

The NIMS document will be reviewed on a 2-year cycle and revised to incorporate new Presidential directives, legislative changes, and procedural changes based on lessons learned from exercises, actual incidents, and planned events. Proposed changes to NIMS will be submitted to the NIC for consideration, approval, and publication.

The Secretary is responsible for publishing revisions and modifications to NIMS-related documents, including supplementary standards, procedures, and other materials, and will do so with regular consultation with other Federal departments and agencies and State and local governments.

3. NIC RESPONSIBILITIES

a. Administration and Compliance

To manage ongoing administration and implementation of NIMS, including specification of compliance measures, the NIC is responsible for working toward the following:

- Developing and maintaining a national program for NIMS education and awareness, including specific instruction on the purpose and content of this document and NIMS in general.

- Promoting compatibility between national-level standards for NIMS and those developed by other public, private, and professional groups.

- Facilitating the establishment and maintenance of a documentation and database system related to qualification, certification, and credentialing of emergency management/response personnel and organizations that includes reviewing and approving discipline-specific requirements (with input from Federal, State, tribal, local, private-sector, nongovernmental, and national professional organizations, as appropriate).

- Developing assessment criteria for the various components of NIMS, as well as compliance requirements and timelines for Federal, State, tribal, and local governments regarding NIMS standards and guidelines.

- Integrating into the national research and development (R&D) agenda—in coordination with the Department of Homeland Security (DHS) Under Secretary for Science and Technology—the NIMS-related science and technology needs of departments, agencies, disciplines, NGOs, and the private sector operating within NIMS.

b. Standards and Credentialing

The NIC will work with appropriate standards development organizations (SDOs) to ensure the adoption of common national standards and credentialing systems that are compatible and aligned with the implementation of NIMS. Identification, adoption, and development of common standards and credentialing programs include the following:

COMPONENT V: ONGOING MANAGEMENT AND MAINTENANCE

- Facilitating the development and publication of national standards, guidelines, and protocols for the qualification, licensure, and certification of emergency management/response personnel, as appropriate.

- Reviewing and approving discipline-specific qualification and certification requirements (with input from Federal, State, tribal, local, nongovernmental, private-sector, and national professional organizations, as appropriate).

- Establishing a data maintenance system to provide incident managers with the detailed qualification, experience, and training information needed to credential personnel for prescribed national incident management positions.

- Coordinating minimum professional certification standards and facilitating the design and implementation of a nationwide credentialing system.

> The NIC recommends that State and local governments <u>voluntarily adopt</u> the following National Fire Protection Association (NFPA) standards: NFPA 1600, "Standard on Disaster/Emergency Management and Business Continuity Programs," and NFPA 1561, "Standard on Emergency Services Incident Management System." These standards, if adopted by the jurisdiction, can assist in NIMS implementation. For information regarding the latest NIC-recommended standards, please visit the NIMS guidance section of the NIC Web site. Other standards may be issued periodically by the NIC and recommended for voluntary adoption.

- Facilitating—with input from Federal, State, tribal, local, nongovernmental, private-sector, and national professional organizations—the establishment of standards for the performance, compatibility, and interoperability of incident management equipment and communications systems, including the following:
    - Facilitating the development and publication of national standards, guidelines, and protocols for equipment certification, including the incorporation of existing standards and certification programs used by incident management and emergency response organizations nationwide.
    - Reviewing and approving lists of equipment that meet these established equipment certification requirements.
    - Collaborating with organizations responsible for emergency-responder equipment evaluation and testing.

- Facilitating the development and issuance of national standards for resource typing.

- Facilitating the definition and maintenance of the information framework required for the development of NIMS information systems, including the development of data standards.

- Coordinating the establishment of technical and technology standards for NIMS users in concert with the DHS Under Secretary for Science and Technology and recognized SDOs.

c. Training and Exercise Support

To lead the development of training and exercises that further appropriate agencies' and organizations' knowledge, adoption, and implementation of NIMS, the NIC will coordinate with them to do the following:

- Facilitate the definition of general training requirements and the development of national-level training standards and course curricula associated with NIMS, including the following:
    - The use of modeling and simulation capabilities for training and exercise programs.
    - Field-based training, specification of mission-essential tasks, requirements for specialized instruction and instructor training, and course completion documentation for all NIMS users.
    - The review and recommendation (in coordination with Federal, State, tribal, local, nongovernmental, private-sector, and national professional organizations) of discipline-specific NIMS training courses.

- Facilitate the development of national standards, guidelines, and protocols for incident management training and exercises, including consideration of existing exercise and training programs at all jurisdictional levels.

- Facilitate the development of training necessary to support the incorporation of NIMS across all jurisdictional levels.

- Establish and maintain a repository for reports and lessons learned from actual incidents, training, and exercises, as well as for best practices, model structures, and processes for NIMS-related functions.

d. Publication Management

Publication management for NIMS includes the development of naming and numbering conventions, the review and certification of publications, development of methods for publications control, identification of sources and suppliers for publications and related services, management of publication distribution, and assurance of product accessibility.[25]

NIMS publication management includes the following types of products:

- Qualifications information.
- Training course and exercise information.
- Task books.
- Incident Command System training, forms, and templates (and other necessary forms).
- Job aids and guides.
- Computer programs.
- Audio and video resources.
- Best-practices manuals/models/recommendations.

---

[25] 47 U.S.C. § 794, Rehabilitation Act of 1973.

To manage NIMS-related publications, the NIC will coordinate with appropriate agencies and organizations and take the lead on the following:

- Facilitating the establishment and maintenance of a publication management system for NIMS-related publications and materials, including the development or coordination of general publications for all NIMS users.

- Issuing documents or information by means of the NIMS publication management system.

- Facilitating the development and publication of standardized templates and materials, such as supplementary documentation and desk guides, to support the implementation and continuous refinement of NIMS.

- Reviewing discipline-specific publication management requirements (with input from Federal, State, tribal, and local governments, as well as nongovernmental, private-sector, and national professional organizations).

B. SUPPORTING TECHNOLOGIES

Ongoing development of science and technology is integral to the continual improvement and refinement of NIMS. Strategic R&D ensures that this development takes place. NIMS also relies on scientifically based technical standards that support incident management. Maintaining a focus on appropriate science and technology solutions will necessitate a long-term collaborative effort among NIMS partners.

To ensure the effective development of incident-management science and technology solutions, the NIC must work in coordination with the DHS Under Secretary for Science and Technology to assess the needs of emergency management/response personnel and their affiliated organizations.

1. CONCEPTS AND PRINCIPLES

NIMS leverages science and technology to improve capabilities and lower costs. It observes the five key principles defined below.

a. Interoperability and Compatibility

Systems operating in an incident management environment must be able to interact smoothly across disciplines and jurisdictions. Interoperability and compatibility are achieved through the use of tools such as common communications and data standards, digital data formats, equipment standards, and design standards.

b. Technology Support

Technology support is the use and incorporation of new and existing technologies to improve efficiency and effectiveness in all aspects of incident management. Technology support permits organizations using NIMS to enhance all aspects of emergency management and incident response. Technology support facilitates incident operations and sustains the R&D programs that underpin the long-term investment in the Nation's future incident management capabilities.

c. Technology Standards

Supporting systems and technologies are based on requirements developed in collaboration with Federal, State, tribal, and local governments, as well as NGOs, the private sector, and national professional organizations. National standards may be required to facilitate the interoperability and compatibility of key systems across jurisdictions and/or disciplines.

d. Broad-Based Requirements

Needs for new technologies, procedures, protocols, and standards to facilitate incident management are identified before, during, and after an incident. As these needs could exceed available resources, NIMS provides a mechanism for aggregating and prioritizing needs and resources. These needs will be met by coordinating testing and evaluation activities for basic, applied, developmental, and demonstration-based research.

e. Strategic R&D Planning

Strategic R&D planning identifies future technologies that can improve or lower the cost of existing incident management capabilities. To ensure effective R&D, the NIC, in coordination with the DHS Under Secretary for Science and Technology, will integrate into the national R&D agenda the incident management science and technology needs of all emergency management/response personnel and their affiliated organizations.

2. SUPPORTING INCIDENT MANAGEMENT WITH SCIENCE AND TECHNOLOGY

Supporting technologies enhance incident management capabilities or lower costs through three principal activities, which are more fully defined below.

a. Operational Scientific Support

Operational scientific support identifies and, on request, mobilizes scientific and technical resources that can be used to support incident management activities. Operational scientific support draws on the scientific and technological expertise of other agencies and organizations. Planning for this category of support is done at each level of government through NIMS preparedness organizations.[26] Operational scientific support is requested and provided through various programs coordinated by DHS and other organizations and agencies.

b. Technical Standards Support

Technical standards support enables the development and coordination of technology standards for NIMS to ensure that personnel, organizations, communications and information systems, and other equipment coordinate and perform consistently, effectively, and reliably without disrupting one another. In coordination with the DHS Science and Technology Directorate, the NIC will coordinate the establishment of technical standards for NIMS users. The following principles will be used in defining these standards:

---

[26] See page 13, Component I: Preparedness, Preparedness Organizations.

COMPONENT V: ONGOING MANAGEMENT AND MAINTENANCE

(1) Performance Measurement

Performance measurement (the collection of "hard" data) is the most reliable basis for standards that ensure the safety and mission effectiveness of emergency responders and incident managers. Within the technology standards process, a performance measurement infrastructure develops guidelines, performance standards, testing protocols, personnel certification, reassessment, and training procedures to help incident management organizations use equipment systems effectively.

(2) Consensus-Based Performance

A consensus-based approach to developing and modifying standards takes advantage of existing SDOs with longstanding interest and expertise in incident management. These SDOs include the National Institute of Justice, National Institute for Standards and Technology, National Institute for Occupational Safety and Health, American National Standards Institute, ASTM International, and NFPA. NIMS, through the NIC, enables working relationships among these SDOs and incident management organizations to develop performance standards for incident management technology.

(3) Testing and Evaluation

NIMS technology criteria will rely on private- and public-sector testing laboratories to evaluate equipment against NIMS technical standards. These organizations will be selected in accordance with guidelines that ensure that testing organizations are both technically proficient and objective (free from conflicting interests) in their testing. The NIC will issue appropriate guidelines as part of its standards development and facilitation responsibilities.

(4) Technical Guidelines for Training Emergency Responders on Equipment Use

Inputs from vulnerability analysts, equipment developers, users, and standards experts are employed to develop scientifically based technical guidelines for training emergency management/response personnel on proper use of equipment. Based on incident management protocols, instruments, and instrument systems, these training guidelines reflect threat and vulnerability information, equipment and systems capabilities, and a range of expected operating conditions. In addition, performance measures and testing protocols developed from these training guidelines provide a repeatable method of measuring the effectiveness of equipment and systems.

c. R&D Support

R&D planning will be based on the operational needs of the entire range of NIMS users. These needs represent key inputs as the Nation formulates its R&D agenda for developing new and improved incident management capabilities. Since operational needs may exceed the resources available for research to address them, these needs must be validated, integrated, and prioritized. DHS is responsible for integrating user needs at all levels into the national R&D agenda.

APPENDIX A:
EXAMPLES OF RESOURCES FOR WHICH TYPING HAS BEEN COMPLETED

As an illustration of how national resource typing is used, Table A-1 shows a single resource that has been completely typed, a Track Dozer. Table A-2 is an example of a team resource that has been completely typed, a Swiftwater/Flood and Rescue Team.

Table A-1. Single Resource (Track Dozer) That Has Been Typed

Resource: Track Dozer						
Category:		Public Works and Engineering (ESF #3)		Kind:		Equipment
Minimum Capabilities:		Type I	Type II	Type III	Type IV	Other
Component	Measures					
Equipment	Example	D10R – Cat 3412E Turbo Charged Diesel	D6N – Cat 3126B Diesel	D3G – Cat 3046 Diesel		D10R WHA (Waste Handling) – Cat 3412E Turbo Charged Diesel
Gross Power	RPM	1,900	2,100	2,400		1,900
Gross Power	kw/hp	457/613	127/170	57/77		457/613
Operating Weight	lbs	144,191	34,209	16,193		144,986
Blade Capacity	yd^3	24.2	5.6	1.88		63.9
Digging Depth	in	26.5	20.5	21.8		26.5
Height	ft/in	6'11"	4'1"	3'.8"		10'5"
Ground Clearance	ft/in	4'11"	3'2.7"			4'10"
Total Tilt	ft/in	3'3"	2'2.2"	1'2.5"		3'6.3"
Width Over End Bits	ft/in	15'11"	10'6"	8'.9"		17'3"
Blade Lift Height	in			27.1		
Digging Depth	in			21.8		
Multishanks Arrangements		1 to 3	3			1 to 3
Ground Clearance Under Tip	in	35	19.9	16.2		35
Machine Ground Clearance	in			14.7		
Max Penetration	in		14.2			37
Max Reach at Ground Line	in		29.1	29.1		

APPENDIX A: EXAMPLES OF RESOURCES FOR WHICH TYPING HAS BEEN COMPLETED

Table A-1. Single Resource (Track Dozer) That Has Been Typed—continued

Resource: Track Dozer						
Category:		Public Works and Engineering (ESF #3)		Kind:		Equipment
Minimum Capabilities:		Type I	Type II	Type III	Type IV	Other
Component	Measures					
Equipment	Example	D10R – Cat 3412E Turbo Charged Diesel	D6N – Cat 3126B Diesel	D3G – Cat 3046 Diesel		D10R WHA (Waste Handling) – Cat 3412E Turbo Charged Diesel
Width	ft/in	9'7"	7'2.7"	8'.9"		9'7"
Winch-Drum Capacity	ft	226	371	371		226
Fuel Capacity	gal	293	79	43.6		293
Max Line Pull Bare Drum	lbs			40,000		
Full Drum	lbs			25,000		
Equipment	Example	D10R	D6N	D3G		D10R WH
Comments:		Caterpillar is used as an example only. The major difference for D10R WHA (Waste Handling) – Cat 3412E Turbo Charged Diesel is that it contains a larger blade and protection guards to prevent landfill type debris from tangling its drives. General Example				

Table A-2. Team Resource (Swiftwater/Flood Search and Rescue Team) That Has Been Typed

Resource: Swiftwater/Flood Search and Rescue Team						
Category:	Search and Rescue				Kind:	Team
Minimum Capabilities:		Type I	Type II	Type III	Type IV
Component	Measure				
Personnel	Team Composition	14-member team: 2 managers 2 squad leaders 10 personnel	6-member team: 1 squad leader 5 personnel	4-member team: 1 squad leader 3 personnel	3-member team: 1 squad leader 2 personnel
Personnel	Minimum number: Technical Animal Rescue	2	1	1	
Personnel	Minimum number: ALS Certified	2			
Personnel	Minimum number: Helicopter/Aquatic Rescue Operations	4	2		
Personnel	Minimum number: Powered Boat Operators	4	2		
Personnel	Minimum number: SCUBA-trained Support Personnel with Equipment	4	2	2	
Personnel	Number and level EMTs	14 EMTs – B 2 EMTs – P	Same as Type III	Same as Type IV	1 EMT – B
Team	Sustained Operations	Same as Type II	24-hour operations	Same as Type IV	18-hour operations
Team	Capabilities	Manage search operations Power vessel operations Helicopter rescue operations Animal rescue HAZMAT ALS Communications Logistics	Manage search operations Power vessel operations Helicopter rescue operations Animal rescue HAZMAT BLS	Assist in search operations Nonpowered watercraft Animal rescue HAZMAT BLS	Low-risk operations Land-based HAZMAT BLS
Team	Specialty S&R Capabilities	Same as Type II	Same as Type III plus: Technical rope systems	In-water contact rescue Dive rescue	

Table A-2. Team Resource (Swiftwater/Flood Search and Rescue Team) That Has Been Typed—continued

Resource: Swiftwater/Flood Search and Rescue Team					
Category:	Search and Rescue			Kind:	Team
Minimum Capabilities:		Type I	Type II	Type III	Type IV
Component	Measure				
Team	Training	Same as Type II except: Divers to have 80 hours of formal public safety diver training	Same as Type III plus: Helicopter operations awareness Technical rope rescue	Same as Type IV plus: Divers to have 60 hours of formal public safety diver training	Class 3 paddle skills Contact and self-rescue skills HAZMAT ICS Swiftwater rescue technician
Team	Certifications	ALS Advanced First Aid & CPR	Same as Type IV	Same as Type IV	BLS Advanced First Aid & CPR
Equipment	Transportation Resources	Equipment trailer, personnel support vehicle			
Personnel	Team Composition	14-member team: 2 managers 2 squad leaders 10 personnel	6-member team: 1 squad leader 5 personnel	4-member team: 1 squad leader 3 personnel	3-member team: 1 squad leader 2 personnel
Equipment	Communication	Same as Type II	Same as Type III plus: Aircraft radio	Same as Type IV plus: Headset	Batteries Portable radios Cell phone
Equipment	Medical	ALS medical kit Blankets Spineboard Litter	Same as Type III plus: Spineboard	Same as Type IV plus: Litter	BLS medical kit Blankets
Equipment	Personal	Same as Type II	Same as Type III plus: Life vests HEED except: PFD Type V	Same as Type IV plus: Fins Lamps	Light sticks; Flares; Markers; Flashlight; Bags; Helmets; Gloves; Knives; PFD Type III/IV; Shoes; Whistles

Table A-2. Team Resource (Swiftwater/Flood Search and Rescue Team) That Has Been Typed—continued

Resource: Swiftwater/Flood Search and Rescue Team						
Category:	Search and Rescue				Kind:	Team
Minimum Capabilities:		Type I	Type II	Type III	Type IV	
Component	Measure					
Equipment	SCUBA	Same as Type III	Same as Type III	SCUBA cylinder Buoyancy compensator Weight belt 2 cutting tools Chest harness & snap shackle Full face mask Underwater communication Dry suit Search line Spare SCUBA cylinder		
Vehicle	Rescue Boat	2 - Fueled	1 - Fueled	1 - Nonpowered 4-person		
Comments:	Conduct search and rescue operations in all water environments, including swiftwater and flood conditions. Water rescue teams come with all team equipment required to conduct operations safely and effectively. For a complete list of recommended training, skills, and equipment, please refer to the FIRESCOPE Swiftwater/Flood Search and Rescue definition at http://www.firescope.org/ics-usar/ICS-SF-SAR-020-1.pdf.					

Note: ALS = advanced life support; EMT = emergency medical technician; BLS = basic life support; CPR = cardiopulmonary resuscitation; HAZMAT = hazardous material; HEED = helicopter emergency egress device; PFD = personal flotation device

APPENDIX B:
INCIDENT COMMAND SYSTEM

A. PURPOSE

Appendix B provides additional explanation and examples relating to the Incident Command System (ICS); this appendix, however, is not a substitute for ICS training.

ICS is used for a broad spectrum of incidents, from routine to complex, both naturally occurring and manmade, by all levels of government—Federal, State, tribal, and local—as well as nongovernmental organizations (NGOs) and the private sector. It is the combination of facilities, equipment, personnel, procedures, and communications operating within a common organizational structure, designed to aid in incident management activities.

Some of the more important "transitional steps" that are necessary to apply ICS in the incident scene environment include the following:

- Recognizing and anticipating the requirement that organizational elements be activated and taking the necessary steps to delegate authority, as appropriate.
- Establishing incident facilities as needed, located to support field operations.
- Establishing the use of common terminology for organizational elements, position titles, facilities, and resources.
- Rapidly evolving from oral direction to the development of a written Incident Action Plan (IAP).

B. ORGANIZATION OF THIS APPENDIX

The major elements of ICS are organized into the following 10 tabs:

- Tab 1—ICS Organization
- Tab 2—The Operations Section
- Tab 3—The Planning Section
- Tab 4—The Logistics Section
- Tab 5—The Finance/Administration Section
- Tab 6—Establishing an Area Command
- Tab 7—Facilities and Locations
- Tab 8—The Planning Process and the IAP
- Tab 9—ICS Forms
- Tab 10—Summary of Major ICS Positions

TAB 1—ICS ORGANIZATION

A. FUNCTIONAL STRUCTURE

The Incident Command System comprises five major functional areas: Command, Operations, Planning, Logistics, and Finance/Administration. (A sixth functional area, Intelligence/Investigations, may be established if required.)

B. MODULAR EXPANSION

The ICS organizational structure is modular, extending to incorporate all elements necessary for the type, size, scope, and complexity of an incident. It builds from the top down; responsibility and performance begin with Incident Command. When the need arises, four separate Sections can be used to organize the General Staff. Each of these Sections may have several subordinate units, or Branches, depending on the incident's management requirements. If one individual can simultaneously manage all major functional areas, no further organization is required. If one or more of the functions requires independent management, an individual is assigned responsibility for that function.

To maintain a manageable span of control, the initial responding Incident Commander (IC) may determine it necessary to delegate functional management to one or more Section Chiefs. The Section Chiefs may further delegate management authority for their areas, as required. A Section Chief may establish Branches, Groups, Divisions, or Units, depending on the Section. Similarly, each functional Unit Leader will further assign individual tasks within the Unit, as needed.

The use of deputies and assistants is a vital part of both the organizational structure and the modular concept. The IC may have one or more deputies, who may be from the same or an assisting agency. Deputies may also be used at Section and Branch levels of the organization. A deputy, whether at the Command, Section, or Branch level, must be fully qualified to assume the position.

The primary reasons to designate a Deputy IC are:

- To perform specific tasks as requested by the IC.
- To perform the incident command function in a relief capacity (e.g., to take over the next operational period; in this case, the deputy will then assume the primary role).
- To represent an assisting agency that may share jurisdiction or have jurisdiction in the future.

Assistants are used as subordinates to the Command Staff, which includes the Public Information Officer, Safety Officer, and Liaison Officer. They have a level of technical capability, qualifications, and responsibility subordinate to the primary positions.
The modular concept described above is based on the following considerations:

- Developing the organization's structure to match the function or task to be performed.
- Staffing only the functional elements required to perform the task.
- Implementing recommended span-of-control guidelines.

- Performing the function of any nonactivated organizational element at the next highest level.
- Deactivating organizational elements no longer required.

For reference, Table B-1 describes the distinctive title assigned to each element of the ICS organization at each corresponding level, as well as the leadership title corresponding to each individual element.

Table B-1. ICS Organization

Organizational Element	Leadership Position Title	Support Positions
Incident Command	Incident Commander	Deputy
Command Staff	Officer	Assistant
Section	Section Chief	Deputy
Branch	Branch Director	Deputy
Divisions and Groups	Supervisors	N/A
Unit	Unit Leader	Manager, Coordinator
Strike Team/Task Force	Leader	Single Resource Boss, Companies/Crews
Single Resource Boss	Boss	N/A
Technical Specialist	Specialist	N/A

1. COMMAND STAFF

In an ICS organization, Incident Command consists of the Incident Commander and various Command Staff positions. The Command Staff are specifically designated, report directly to the Incident Commander, and are assigned responsibility for key activities that are not a part of the General Staff functional elements. Three staff positions are typically identified in ICS: Public Information Officer, Safety Officer, and Liaison Officer. Additional positions may be required, such as technical specialists, depending on the nature, scope, complexity, and location(s) of the incident(s), or according to specific requirements established by the IC.

a. Public Information Officer

The Public Information Officer is responsible for interfacing with the public and media and with other agencies with incident-related information requirements. The Public Information Officer assembles accurate, accessible, and complete information on the incident's cause, size, and current situation; the resources committed; and other matters of general interest for both internal and external audiences. The Public Information Officer may also perform a key public information-monitoring role, such as implementing measures for rumor control. Whether the command structure is single or unified, only one Public Information Officer should be designated per incident. Assistants may be assigned from other involved departments or agencies. The IC must approve the release of all incident-related information. In large-scale incidents or where multiple command posts are established, the

Public Information Officer should participate in or lead the Joint Information Center in order to ensure consistency in the provision of information to the public.

b. Safety Officer

The Safety Officer monitors incident operations and advises Incident Command on all matters relating to operational safety, including the health and safety of emergency responder personnel. The ultimate responsibility for the safe conduct of incident management operations rests with the IC or Unified Command (UC) and supervisors at all levels of incident management. In turn, the Safety Officer is responsible for developing the Incident Safety Plan—the set of systems and procedures necessary to ensure ongoing assessment of hazardous environments, coordination of multiagency safety efforts, and implementation of measures to promote emergency management/incident personnel safety, as well as the general safety of incident operations. The Safety Officer has emergency authority to stop and/or prevent unsafe acts during incident operations.

In a UC structure, a single Safety Officer should be designated regardless of the involvement of multiple jurisdictions or functional agencies. The Safety Officer, Operations Section Chief, Planning Section Chief, and Logistics Section Chief must coordinate closely regarding operational safety and emergency responder health and safety issues. The Safety Officer must also ensure the coordination of safety management functions and issues across jurisdictions, across functional agencies, and with NGOs and the private sector.

It is important to note that the agencies, organizations, or jurisdictions that contribute to joint safety management efforts do not lose their individual identities or responsibility for their own programs, policies, and personnel. Rather, each contributes to the overall effort to protect all responder personnel involved in incident operations.

Assistant Safety Officers may be assigned from departments or agencies constituting the UC. Some types of incidents, such as a hazardous materials incident, require Assistant Safety Officers to have special skill sets. The Assistant Safety Officer positions described below are examples of such positions, and Figure B-1 illustrates how the Safety Officer and example Assistant Safety Officers could be positioned in an incident.

- The Assistant Safety Officer for hazardous materials would be assigned to carry out the functions outlined in 29 CFR 1910.120 (Hazardous Waste Operations and Emergency Response). This person should have the required knowledge, skills, and abilities to provide oversight for specific hazardous material operations at the field level.
- The Assistant Safety Officer for fire would be assigned to assist the Branch Director providing oversight for specific fire operations. This person would have the required knowledge, skills, and abilities to provide this function.
- The Assistant Safety Officer for food would be assigned to the Food Unit to provide oversight of food handling and distribution. This person would have the required knowledge, skills, and abilities to provide this function. An example would be a food specialist from a local health department.

**Figure B-1. Example of the Role of Safety Officer and
Assistant Safety Officers in ICS in a Multibranch Incident**

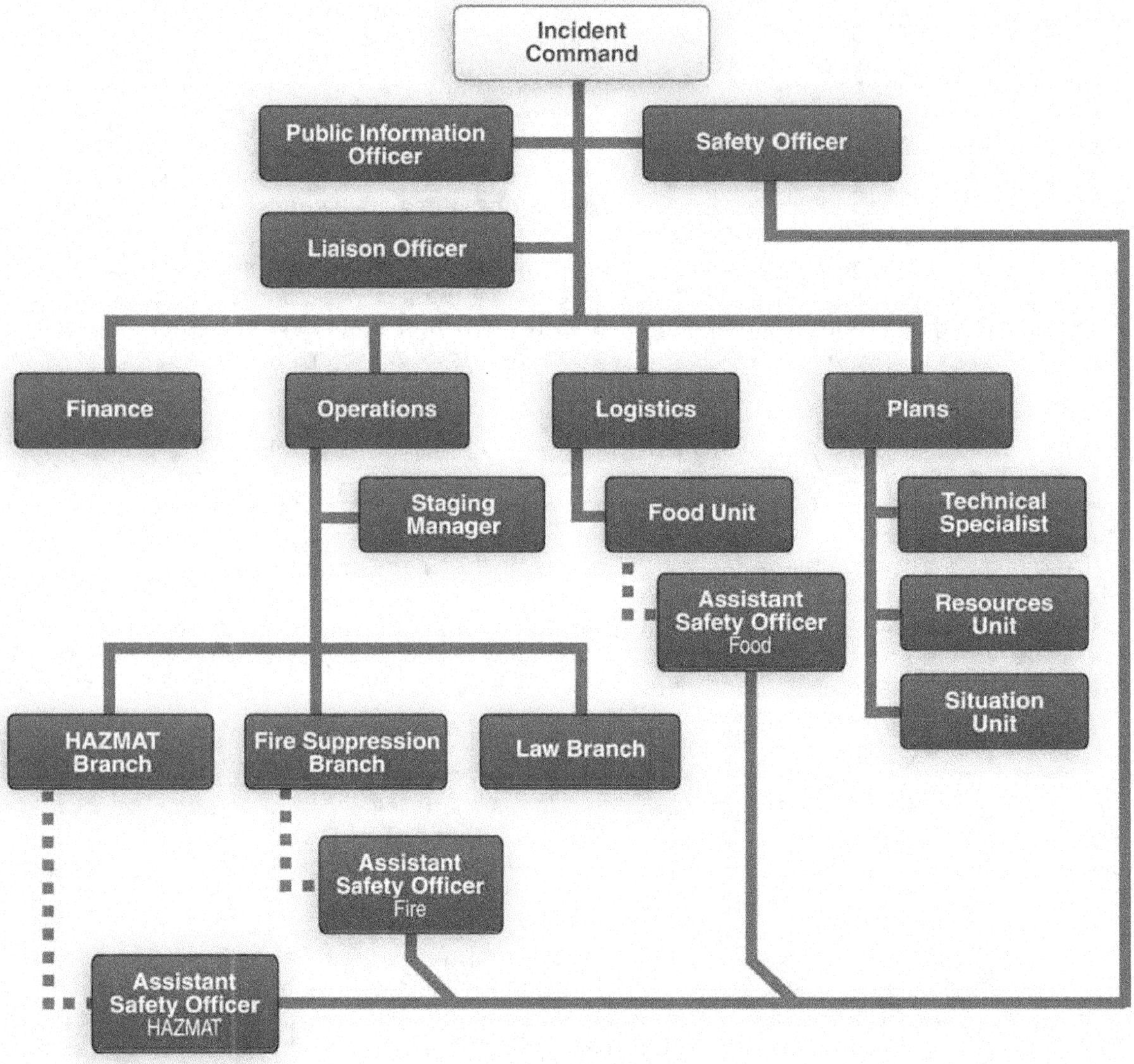

The dotted-line connections represent coordination and communication between the two points, not necessarily a direct link within the chain of command.

c. Liaison Officer

The Liaison Officer is Incident Command's point of contact for representatives of other governmental departments and agencies, NGOs, and/or the private sector (with no jurisdiction or legal authority) to provide input on their organization's policies, resource availability, and other incident-related matters. In either a single or unified command structure, representatives from assisting or cooperating organizations coordinate through the Liaison Officer. Organizational representatives assigned to an incident must have the authority to speak for their parent agencies and/or organizations on all matters, following appropriate consultations with their agency leadership. Assistants and personnel from NGOs and the private sector involved in incident management activities may be assigned to the Liaison Officer to facilitate coordination.

d. Additional Command Staff

Additional Command Staff positions may also be necessary depending on the nature and location(s) of the incident, or specific requirements established by Incident Command. For example, a legal counsel may be assigned to the Planning Section as a technical specialist or directly to the Command Staff to advise Incident Command on legal matters, such as emergency proclamations, legality of evacuation orders, isolation and quarantine, and legal rights and restrictions pertaining to media access. Similarly, a medical advisor may be designated and assigned directly to the Command Staff to provide advice and recommendations to Incident Command in the context of incidents involving medical and mental health services, mass casualty response, acute care, vector control, epidemiology, or mass prophylaxis considerations, particularly in the response to a bioterrorism incident.

APPENDIX B: INCIDENT COMMAND SYSTEM

TAB 2—THE OPERATIONS SECTION

The Operations Section is responsible for managing operations directed toward reducing the immediate hazard at the incident site, saving lives and property, establishing situation control, and restoring normal conditions. Incidents can include acts of terrorism, wildland and urban fires, floods, hazardous material spills, nuclear accidents, aircraft accidents, earthquakes, hurricanes, tornadoes, tropical storms, war-related disasters, public health and medical emergencies, and other incidents requiring an emergency response.

Because of its functional management structure, ICS is applicable across a spectrum of incidents differing in size, scope, and complexity. The types of agencies that could be included in the Operations Section include fire, law enforcement, public health, public works, and emergency services. Depending on the situation, these agencies may work together as a unit or in various combinations. Many incidents may involve government agencies, NGOs, and the private sector as partners in the Operations Section.

Incident operations can be organized and executed in many ways. The specific method selected will depend on the type of incident, the agencies involved, and the objectives and strategies of the incident management effort. The following discussion presents several different methods of organizing tactical operations in response to an incident. In some cases, the approach will be strictly functional. In other cases, a method will be selected to accommodate jurisdictional boundaries. In still others, a mix of functional and geographical approaches may be appropriate. While ICS organizational management is directly correlated with the size and complexity of the incident, the need to maintain a manageable span of control for all resources means that the number of subordinate units or single resources is what drives the functions of ICS. ICS offers extensive flexibility in determining the appropriate approach using the factors described above.

A. OPERATIONS SECTION CHIEF

The Operations Section Chief directly manages all incident tactical activities and implements the IAP. The Operations Section Chief may have one or more deputies, preferably from other agencies in multijurisdictional incidents. An Operations Section Chief should be designated for each operational period and will have direct involvement in the development of the IAP for the next operational period of responsibility.

B. BRANCHES

Branches may be established to meet several challenges:

1. Maintaining Recommended Span of Control for the Operations Section Chief

The recommended span of control for the Operations Section Chief is 1:5—as for all managers and supervisory personnel—or as high as 1:10 for larger scale law enforcement operations. When this is exceeded, the Operations Section Chief should set up two Branches (see Figure B-2), allocating the Divisions and Groups between them. For example, if one Group and four Divisions are reporting to the Operations Section Chief, and two Divisions and one Group are to be added, a two-Branch organization may be formed.

The type of incident, nature of the task, hazards and safety factors, and distances between personnel and resources all have an influence on span-of-control considerations.

Figure B-2. Geographic Branch Organization

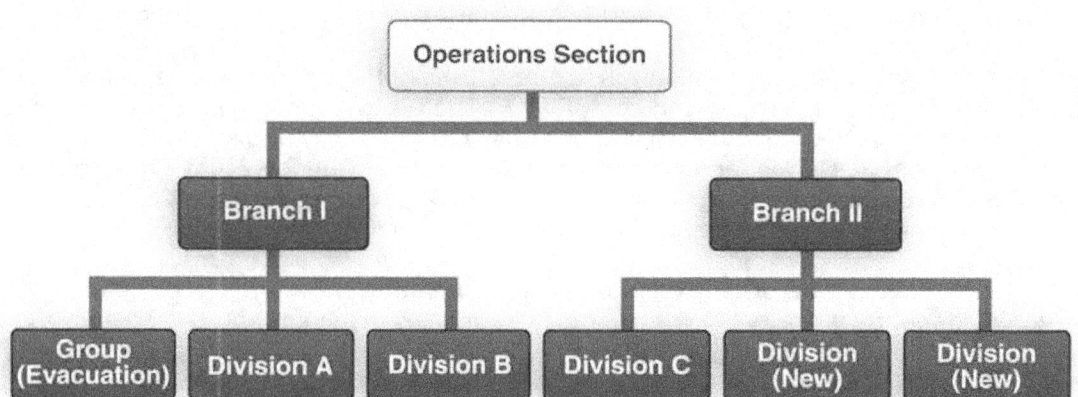

2. Incident Calls for a Functional Branch Structure

A functional Branch structure can be illustrated through an example: If a large aircraft crashes in a city, various departments within the city (including police, fire, emergency services, and public health services) might each have a functional Branch operating under the direction of a single Operations Section Chief. In this example (shown in Figure B-3), the Operations Section Chief is from the fire department, with deputies from police and emergency medical services (EMS). Other alignments could be made, depending on the city plan and type of emergency. Note that, in this situation, the command structure could be either single or unified, depending on the jurisdiction.

Figure B-3. Deputy Operations With Functional Branch Structure

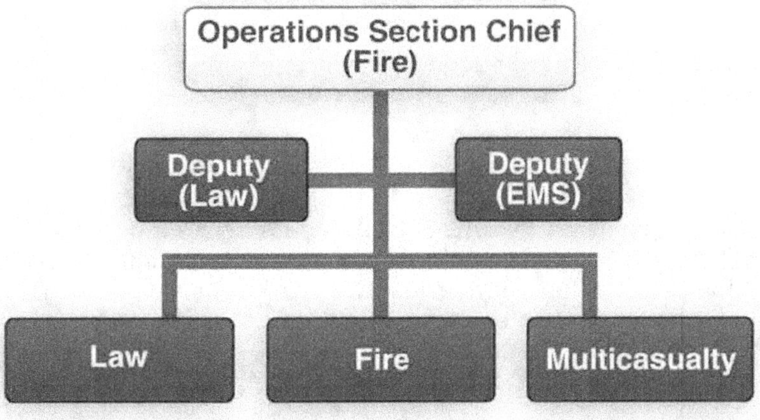

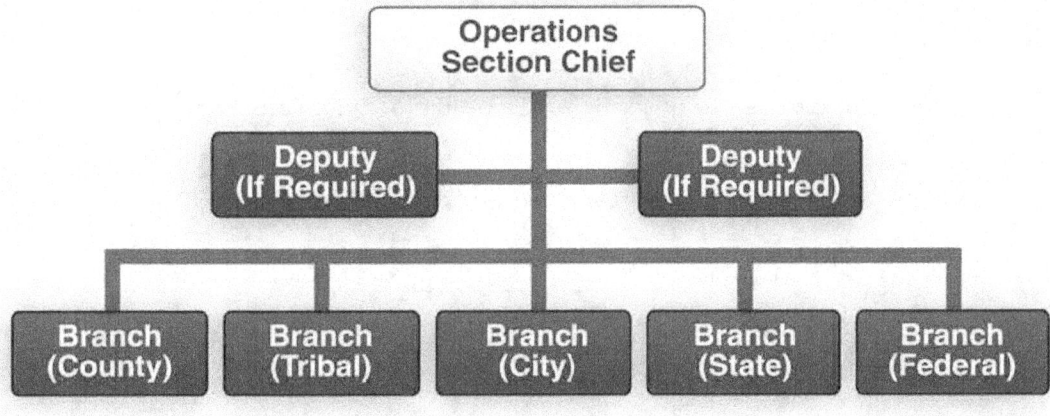

3. Incident Calls for a Multijurisdictional Branch Structure

The response to a major flood might require combining Federal, State, tribal, and local resources. In this case, resources are best managed under the agencies that normally control them, creating a multijurisdictional Branch structure, as illustrated in Figure B-4.

Figure B-4. Multijurisdictional Incident

C. DIVISIONS AND GROUPS

Divisions and Groups are established when the number of resources exceeds the Operations Section Chief's manageable span of control. Divisions separate physical or geographical areas of operation within the incident area. Groups separate functional areas of operation for the incident.

The use of the two terms is necessary, because *Division* always refers to a geographical assignment and *Group* always refers to a functional assignment. Both Divisions and Groups may be used in a single incident. Maintaining proper coordination is vital to the success of these operations.

As additional types of resources are added to the organization, resources should be assigned into a Division structure.

1. Geographical Divisions

One way to create geographical Divisions is to separate an area according to natural terrain boundaries or other prominent geographical features, such as rivers. When geographical features are used for determining boundaries, the size of the Division should correspond to appropriate span-of-control guidelines (see Figure B-5).

Figure B-5. Use of Geographical Divisions

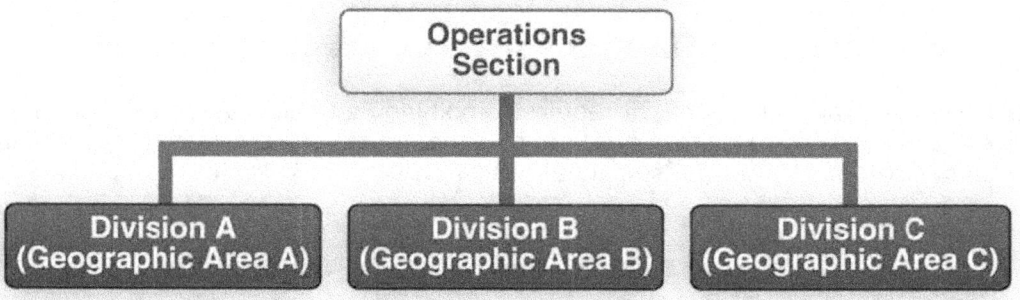

2. Functional Groups

Functional Groups can be used to describe areas of like activity (e.g., rescue, evacuation, or medical), as shown in Figure B-6.

Figure B-6. Use of Functional Groups

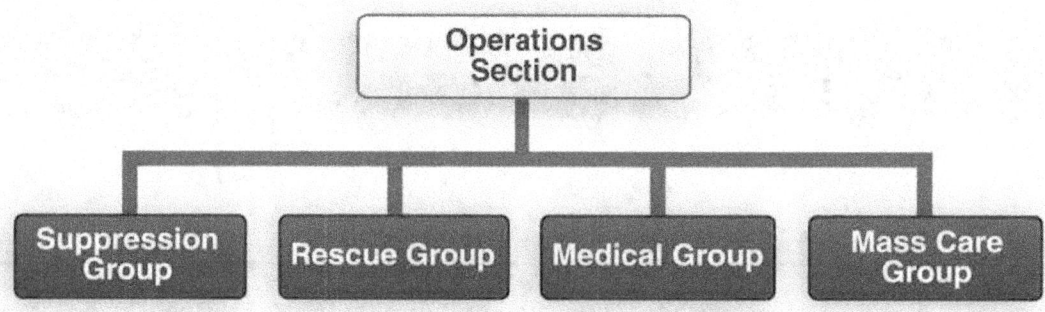

3. Combined Geographical Divisions and Functional Groups

It is also possible to have both Divisions and Groups within the Operations Section. For example, Divisions A, B, and C (based on geographical locations) may work in conjunction with functional Groups assigned to specific tasks (e.g., traffic control and smoke ventilation) in those locations. Alternatively, Groups may be assigned throughout the entire incident and may work independently or in conjunction with Divisions. Organizationally, the Supervisors of Divisions and Groups have the same level of authority.

D. RESOURCE ORGANIZATION

Initially, in any incident, responding individual resources (single resources, Strike Teams, and Task Forces) will report directly to the IC/UC. Task Forces and Strike Teams are an effective way to reduce the span of control over a large number of single resources. As the incident grows in size or complexity, these individual resources may operate within Divisions and/or Groups.

1. Single Resources

Resources may be employed on a single basis, such as individual personnel, equipment, and any associated operators. This is typically the case in the context of the initial response to the incident.

2. Task Forces

Task Forces are any combination of resources convened to accomplish a specific mission and can be ad hoc or planned. Task Forces include a designated leader and operate with common communications. Several key resource elements can be managed under one individual's supervision, thus aiding in span of control. As an example, during a flood incident, a public works Task Force might be established, with the mission of opening storm drains. It might consist of a dump truck, a backhoe, a front loader, a five-person crew with shovels and transportation, and a Task Force Leader (e.g., public works foreman with vehicle and communications).

3. Strike Teams

A Strike Team consists of a set number of resources of the same kind and type operating under a designated leader with common communications between them. Strike Teams represent known capability and are highly effective management units. As an example, for a fire response a Strike Team could consist of five Type I engines and a Strike Team Leader. The Strike Team Leader is required to have a vehicle with communication capabilities to communicate with his or her team.

E. AIR OPERATIONS BRANCH

The Operations Section Chief may establish an Air Operations Branch and designate its director, when the complexity of air operations requires additional support and effort or when the incident requires mixing tactical and logistical utilization of helicopters and other aircraft. Aviation safety is a paramount concern in complex operations, and a designated Air Operations Branch ensures the safe and efficient use of aviation resources. Figure B-7 shows a typical organizational structure for air operations.

Whenever helicopters and fixed-wing aircraft must operate simultaneously within the incident airspace, an Air Tactical Group Supervisor should be designated. This individual coordinates all airborne activity with the assistance of a helicopter coordinator and a fixed-wing coordinator. When only one helicopter is used, however, the helicopter may be directly under the control of the Operations Section Chief.

The Air Support Group establishes and operates bases for rotary-wing air assets and maintains required liaison with off-incident fixed-wing bases. The Air Support Group is responsible for all timekeeping for aviation resources assigned to the incident.

Figure B-7. Air Operations Organization

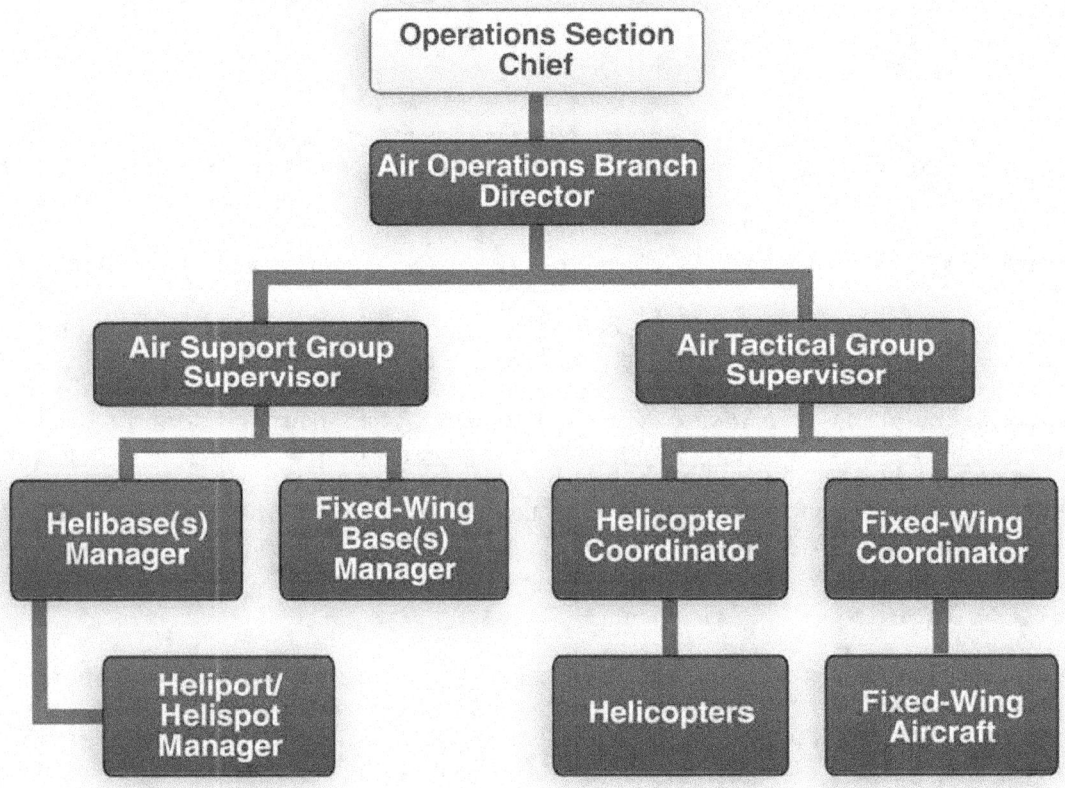

TAB 3—THE PLANNING SECTION

The Planning Section is responsible for collecting, evaluating, and disseminating operational information pertaining to the incident. This Section maintains information and intelligence on the current and forecasted situation, as well as the status of resources assigned to the incident. The Planning Section prepares and documents Incident Action Plans and incident maps, and gathers and disseminates information and intelligence critical to the incident. The Planning Section has four primary Units and may also include technical specialists to assist in evaluating the situation and forecasting requirements for additional personnel and equipment.

A. PLANNING SECTION CHIEF

The Planning Section Chief oversees all incident-related data gathering and analysis regarding incident operations and assigned resources, conducts Planning Meetings, and prepares the IAP for each operational period. This individual will normally come from the jurisdiction with primary incident responsibility and may have one or more deputies from other participating jurisdictions.

B. RESOURCES UNIT

1. Responsibilities

The Resources Unit makes certain that all assigned personnel and resources have checked in at the incident. Resources consist of personnel, teams, crews, aircraft, and equipment available for assignment to or employment during an incident. The Resources Unit maintains a system for keeping track of the current location and status of all assigned resources and maintains a master list of all resources committed to incident operations.

2. Resource Status

Resources must be categorized by kind and type (capability and capacity), and resource status must be tracked continuously to manage them effectively during an incident. The following status conditions and procedures are used for maintaining an up-to-date and accurate picture of resource status.

a. Status Conditions

Tactical resources at an incident can have one of three status conditions:

- ***Assigned:*** Resources that are checked in and are cleared to work on an incident.
- ***Available:*** Personnel, teams, equipment, or facilities that have been assigned to an incident and are ready for a specific work detail or function.
- ***Out of Service:*** Assigned resources that are unable to function for mechanical, personal, or health reasons.

b. Changes in Status

Typically, when the status of a resource has changed (e.g., a unit that was previously listed as "out of service" is reclassified as "available"), the Unit Leader or the supervisor who approved the status change should immediately notify the Resources Unit Leader, who, in turn, will make the appropriate status reclassification.

C. SITUATION UNIT

The Situation Unit collects, processes, and organizes ongoing situation information; prepares situation summaries; and develops projections and forecasts of future events related to the incident. The Situation Unit prepares maps and also gathers and disseminates information and intelligence for use in the IAP. This Unit should be prepared to provide timely situation reports as scheduled or at the request of the Planning Section Chief or IC. This Unit may also require the expertise of technical specialists.

D. DOCUMENTATION UNIT

The Documentation Unit maintains accurate and complete incident files, including a complete record of the major steps taken to resolve the incident; provides duplication services to incident personnel; and files, maintains, and stores incident files for legal, analytical, and historical purposes. This Unit compiles and publishes the IAP and maintains the files and records that are developed as part of the overall IAP and planning function.

E. DEMOBILIZATION UNIT

The Demobilization Unit develops an Incident Demobilization Plan that includes specific instructions for all personnel and resources that will require demobilization. This Unit should begin its work early in the incident, creating rosters of personnel and resources, and obtaining any missing information as check-in proceeds. Note that many city- and county-provided resources are local, and as such do not require specific demobilization instructions. Once the Incident Demobilization Plan has been approved, the Demobilization Unit ensures that it is distributed both at the incident and elsewhere as necessary.

F. TECHNICAL SPECIALISTS

ICS is designed to function in a wide variety of incident scenarios that require the use of technical specialists. These personnel have special skills and are activated only when needed. Specialists may serve anywhere within the organization, including the Command Staff. No specific incident qualifications are prescribed or required, as technical specialists normally perform the same duties during an incident that they perform in their everyday jobs, and they are typically certified in their fields or professions.

Technical specialists are most often assigned to the specific area (Section, Branch, Unit, Division, etc.) where their services are needed and performed. In some situations they may be assigned to a separate Unit within the Planning Section, much like a talent pool, and assigned out to various jobs on a temporary basis. For example, a tactical specialist may be sent to the Operations Section to assist with tactical matters, a financial specialist may be sent to the Finance/Administration Section to assist with fiscal matters, or a legal specialist or legal counsel may be assigned directly to the Command Staff to advise the IC/UC on legal matters, such as emergency proclamations, legality of evacuation orders, isolation and quarantine, and legal rights and restrictions pertaining to media access. Generally, if the expertise is needed for only a short period and involves only one individual, that individual should be assigned to the Situation Unit. If the expertise will be required on a long-term basis and requires several persons, it is advisable to establish a separate Technical Unit in the Planning Section.

A specific example of the need to establish a distinct Technical Unit within the General Staff is the requirement to coordinate and manage large volumes of environmental samples or analytical data from multiple sources in the context of certain complex incidents, particularly those involving biological, chemical, or radiological hazards. To meet this requirement, an Environmental Unit could be established within the Planning Section to facilitate interagency environmental data managing, monitoring, sampling, analyzing, and assessing. The Environmental Unit would prepare environmental data for the Situation Unit and work in close coordination with other Units and Sections within the ICS structure to enable effective decision support to the IC or UC. Technical specialists assigned to the Environmental Unit might include a scientific support coordinator as well as technicians proficient in response technologies, weather forecast, resources at risk, sampling, cleanup assessment, and disposal.

Examples of Technical Specialists

Agricultural specialist
Chemical or radiological decontamination specialist
Communication specialist
Cultural resource specialist
Data management specialist
Emergency medical services specialist
Environmental impact specialist
Epidemiologist
Explosives specialist
Faith community representative
Firefighter specialist
Flood control specialist
Forensic pathologist
Hazardous materials technician
Homeland security specialist
Industrial hygienist
Intelligence specialist
Law enforcement specialist
Legal counsel
Mass care specialist
Meteorologist
Military specialist
Mortuary affairs specialist
Numerical modeler
Occupational safety and health specialist
Pharmacist
Public health specialist
Public relations specialist
Radiation health specialist
Records management specialist
Resource/cost specialist
Scientific support coordinator
Special needs advisor
Structural engineering specialist
Toxicologist
Transportation specialist
Veterinarian
Waste management specialist
Water-use specialist

Tasks accomplished by the Environmental Unit might include the following:

- Identifying sensitive areas and recommending response priorities.
- Developing a plan for collecting, transporting, and analyzing samples.
- Providing input on wildlife protection strategies.
- Determining the extent and effects of site contamination.
- Developing site cleanup and hazardous material disposal plans.
- Identifying the need for and obtaining permits and other authorizations.

TAB 4—THE LOGISTICS SECTION

The Logistics Section provides for all the support needs for the incident, such as ordering resources and providing facilities, transportation, supplies, equipment maintenance and fuel, food service, communications, and medical services for incident personnel.

The Logistics Section is led by a Section Chief, who may also have one or more deputies. Having a deputy is encouraged when all designated Units are established at an incident site. When the incident is very large or requires a number of facilities with large numbers of equipment, the Logistics Section can be divided into Branches. This helps with span of control by providing more effective supervision and coordination among the individual Units. Conversely, in smaller incidents or when fewer resources are needed, a Branch configuration may be used to combine the task assignments of individual Units. Figure B-8 provides an example of the Logistics Section organized with Service and Support Branches.

Figure B-8. Logistics Section With Branch Organizational Structure

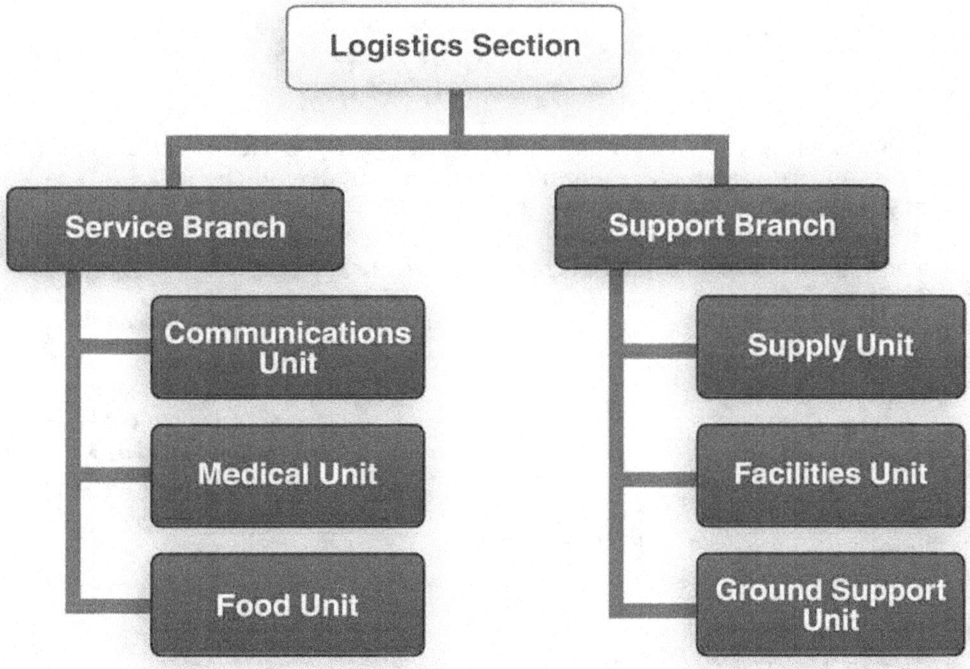

A. SUPPLY UNIT

The Supply Unit orders, receives, processes, stores, inventories, and distributes all incident-related resources and supplies.

Once established, the Supply Unit also has the basic responsibility for all off-incident ordering, including the following:

- All tactical and support resources (including personnel).
- All expendable and nonexpendable supplies required for incident support.

The Supply Unit provides the support required to receive, process, store, and distribute all supply orders. The Unit also handles tool operations, which includes storing, disbursing, and servicing tools and portable, nonexpendable equipment. Additionally, the Supply Unit assists in projecting resource needs based on information provided in the IAP.

B. FACILITIES UNIT

The Facilities Unit sets up, maintains, and demobilizes all facilities used in support of incident operations. The Unit also provides facility maintenance and law enforcement/security services required for incident support.

The Facilities Unit sets up the Incident Command Post (ICP), Incident Base, and Camps (including trailers or other forms of shelter for use in and around the incident area); it also provides the services associated with maintaining those functions. The Incident Base and Camps may be established in areas having existing structures, which are used in whole or in part. The Facilities Unit also provides and sets up necessary personnel support facilities, including areas for the following:

- Food and hydration service.
- Sleeping.
- Sanitation and showers.
- Staging.

This Unit also orders, through Supply, such additional support items as portable toilets, shower facilities, and lighting units.

> Providing shelter for victims is a critical operational activity, which should be incorporated into the IAP. Sheltering is normally conducted by appropriate nongovernmental organization staff, such as the American Red Cross or other similar entities.

C. GROUND SUPPORT UNIT

The Ground Support Unit:

- Maintains and repairs primary tactical vehicles and mobile ground support equipment.
- Records usage time for all ground equipment (including contract equipment) assigned to the incident.
- Supplies fuel for all mobile equipment.
- Provides transportation in support of incident operations (except aircraft).
- Develops and implements the incident Traffic Plan.

In addition to its primary functions of maintaining and servicing vehicles and mobile equipment, the Ground Support Unit maintains a transportation pool for major incidents. This pool consists of vehicles (e.g., staff cars, buses, or pickups) that are suitable for transporting personnel. The Ground Support Unit also provides to the Resources Unit up-to-date information on the location and status of transportation vehicles assigned to the Ground Support Unit.

D. COMMUNICATIONS UNIT

The Communications Unit develops the Communications Plan (ICS 205), to make the most effective use of the communications equipment and facilities assigned to the incident. Additionally, this Unit installs and tests all communications equipment, supervises and operates the incident communications center, distributes and recovers communications equipment assigned to incident personnel, and maintains and repairs communications equipment on site.

The Communications Unit is responsible for effective incident communications planning, especially in the context of a multiagency incident. All communications between organizational elements during an incident should be in plain language (clear text) to ensure that information dissemination is clear and understood by all intended recipients. Planning is critical for determining required radio nets, establishing interagency frequency assignments, and ensuring the interoperability and the optimal use of all assigned communications capabilities.

The Communications Unit Leader should attend all incident Planning Meetings to ensure that the communication systems available for the incident can support tactical operations planned for the next operational period.

Incident communications are managed through the use of an incident Communications Plan and a communications center established solely for the use of tactical and support resources assigned to the incident.

Advance planning is required to ensure that an appropriate communications system is available to support incident operations requirements. This planning includes the development of frequency inventories, frequency-use agreements, and interagency radio caches.

Most complex incidents will require a Communications Plan. The Communications Unit is responsible for planning the use of radio frequencies; establishing networks for command, tactical, support, and air units; setting up on-scene telephone and public address equipment; and providing any required off-incident communication links. Codes should not be used for radio communication. A clear spoken message—based on common terminology that avoids misunderstanding in complex and noisy situations—reduces the chances for error. The use of common terminology allows emergency management/response personnel to communicate clearly with one another and effectively coordinate activities, no matter the size, scope, location, or complexity of the incident.

Radio networks for large incidents may be organized as follows:

1. Command Net

The command net links together Incident Command, Command Staff, Section Chiefs, Branch Directors, and Division and Group Supervisors.

2. Tactical Nets

Several tactical nets may be established to connect departments, agencies, geographical areas, or specific functional units. The determination of how nets are set up should be a joint function designed by Planning, Operations, and Logistics.

3. Support Net

A support net may be established primarily to handle changes in resource status but also to handle logistical requests and other nontactical functions.

4. Air-to-Ground Net

To coordinate air-to-ground traffic, either a specific tactical frequency may be designated, or regular tactical nets may be used.

5. Air-to-Air Nets

Air-to-air nets may be designated and assigned for use at the incident. An air-to-air net is designed to be used by airborne assets; ground units should not utilize this net.

E. FOOD UNIT

The Food Unit determines food and hydration requirements of the responders, and has the responsibility for planning menus, ordering food, providing cooking facilities, cooking and serving food, maintaining food service areas, and managing food security and safety.

Efficient food service is important, but it is especially important for any extended incident. The Food Unit must be able to anticipate incident needs, such as the number of people who will need to be fed and whether the type, location, or complexity of the incident predicates special food requirements. The Unit must supply food needs for the entire incident, including all remote locations (e.g., Camps and Staging Areas), and also supply food service to operations personnel who are unable to leave their assignments.

> Feeding affected nonresponse persons (e.g., victims, evacuees, persons at shelters) is a critical operational activity that will normally be incorporated into the IAP. Feeding activities will normally be conducted by members of appropriate NGOs, such as the American Red Cross or similar entities. Services provided by appropriate NGOs would not fall within the Food Unit but in a separate functional assignment that should be communicated and coordinated with the IC and Operations Section Chief to ensure operational continuity.

The Food Unit must interact closely with the following elements:

- Planning Section, to determine the number of personnel who must be fed.
- Facilities Unit, to arrange food service areas.
- Supply Unit, to order food, unless provided under contract or agreement.
- Ground Support Unit, to obtain ground transportation.
- Air Operations Branch Director, to deliver food to remote locations.

Careful planning and monitoring is required to ensure food safety before and during food service operations, including the assignment, as indicated, of public health professionals with expertise in environmental health and food safety.

F. MEDICAL UNIT

The Medical Unit is responsible for the effective and efficient provision of medical services to incident personnel, and reports directly to the Logistics Section Chief. The primary responsibilities of the Medical Unit include the following:

> Patient care and medical services for those who are not emergency management/response personnel (e.g., incident victims) are critical operational activities. These activities are incorporated into the IAP as key considerations and should be staffed accordingly with appropriate professional personnel.

- Develop procedures for handling any major medical emergency involving incident personnel.
- Develop the Incident Medical Plan (for incident personnel).
- Provide continuity of medical care, including vaccinations, vector control, occupational health, prophylaxis, and mental health services for incident personnel.
- Provide transportation for injured incident personnel.
- Coordinate and establish the routine rest and rehabilitation of incident responders.
- Ensure that injured incident personnel are tracked as they move from their origin to a care facility and from there to final disposition.
- Assist in processing all paperwork related to injuries or deaths of incident-assigned personnel.
- Coordinate personnel and mortuary affairs for incident personnel fatalities.

The Medical Unit Leader will develop a Medical Plan, which will, in turn, form part of the IAP. The Medical Plan should provide specific information on medical assistance capabilities at incident locations, potentially hazardous areas or conditions, and off-site medical assistance facilities and procedures for handling complex medical emergencies. The Medical Unit will also assist the Finance/Administration Section with the administrative requirements related to injury compensation, including obtaining written authorizations, billing forms, witness statements, administrative medical documents, and reimbursement as required. The Medical Unit will ensure patient privacy to the fullest extent possible.

TAB 5—THE FINANCE/ ADMINISTRATION SECTION

A Finance/Administration Section is established when there is a specific need for financial and/or administrative services to support incident management activities. Large or evolving scenarios involve significant funding originating from multiple sources. In addition to monitoring multiple sources of funds, the Section Chief must track and report to the IC/UC the accrued cost as the incident progresses. This allows the IC/UC to forecast the need for additional funds before operations are affected negatively, and it is particularly important if significant operational resources are under contract from the private sector.

> While the functions of Finance/Administration are critical components of effective command and management, components of the Finance/Administration Section are not necessarily staffed on the incident scene. Wireless communications systems enable some of the Finance/Administration functions to be performed away from the incident scene, typically in the workstations where these functions would customarily be performed.

The Section Chief may also need to monitor expenditures to ensure that applicable statutory rules are met. Close coordination with the Planning and Logistics Sections is essential so that operational records can be reconciled with financial documents.

The Finance/Administration Section Chief will determine, given current and anticipated future requirements, the need for establishing specific subordinate units. Because of the specialized nature of finance functions, the Section Chief should come from the agency that has the greatest requirement for this support. The Finance/Administration Section Chief may also have one or more deputies.

A. TIME UNIT

The Time Unit is responsible primarily for ensuring proper daily recording of personnel time, in accordance with the policies of the relevant agencies. The Time Unit also ensures that the Logistics Section records or captures equipment-use time.

If applicable (depending on the agencies involved), personnel time records will be collected and processed for each operational period. The Time Unit Leader may require the assistance of personnel familiar with the relevant policies of any affected agencies. These records must be verified, checked for accuracy, and posted according to existing policies. Excess hours worked must also be determined, for which separate logs must be maintained.

B. PROCUREMENT UNIT

The Procurement Unit administers all financial matters pertaining to vendor contracts. This Unit coordinates with local jurisdictions to identify sources for equipment, prepares and signs equipment rental agreements, and processes all administrative requirements associated with equipment rental and supply contracts. In some cases, the Supply Unit in the Logistics Section will be responsible for certain procurement activities. The Procurement Unit will also work closely with local cost authorities.

C. COMPENSATION AND CLAIMS UNIT

Under ICS, a single Unit handles injury compensation and claims. Depending on the incident, the specific activities are varied and may not always be accomplished by the same person. The individual handling injury compensation ensures that all forms required by workers' compensation programs and local agencies are completed. This individual also maintains files on injuries and illnesses associated with the incident, and ensures that all witness statements are obtained in writing. Since the Medical Unit may also perform some of these tasks, close coordination between the Medical and Compensation and Claims Units is essential. The claims function handles investigations of all civil tort claims involving property associated with or involved in the incident. The Compensation and Claims Unit maintains logs on the claims, obtains witness statements, and documents investigations and agency followup requirements.

D. COST UNIT

The Cost Unit provides cost analysis data for the incident. This Unit must ensure that equipment and personnel for which payment is required are properly identified, obtain and record all cost data, and analyze and prepare estimates of incident costs. The Cost Unit also provides input on cost estimates for resource use to the Planning Section. The Cost Unit must maintain accurate information on the actual costs of all assigned resources.

TAB 6—ESTABLISHING AN AREA COMMAND

As described in the Command and Management component, the purpose of an Area Command is either to oversee the management of multiple incidents that are each being handled by a separate ICS organization or to oversee the management of a very large or evolving incident that has multiple Incident Management Teams (IMTs) engaged.

A. RESPONSIBILITIES

The Area Command does not have operational responsibilities. For the incidents under its authority, the Area Command:

- Develops broad objectives for the impacted area(s).
- Coordinates the development of individual incident objectives and strategies.
- (Re)allocates resources as the established priorities change.
- Ensures that incidents are properly managed.
- Ensures effective communications.
- Ensures that incident management objectives are met and do not conflict with each other or with agency policies.
- Identifies critical resource needs and reports them to the established EOCs/Multiagency Coordination Groups.
- Ensures that short-term "emergency" recovery is coordinated to assist in the transition to full recovery operations.

The function of Area Command is to develop broad objectives for the impacted area and to coordinate the development of individual incident objectives and strategies. Additionally, the Area Commander will set priorities for the use of critical resources allocated to the incident.

B. ORGANIZATION

The Area Command organization operates under the same basic principles as ICS. Typically, an Area Command will comprise the following key personnel, all of whom must possess appropriate qualifications and certifications:

1. Area Commander (Unified Area Command)

The Area Commander is responsible for the overall direction of the IMTs assigned. This responsibility includes ensuring that conflicts are resolved, incident objectives established, and strategies selected for the use of critical resources. The Area Commander is also responsible for coordinating with Federal, State, tribal, and local departments and agencies, as well as NGOs and the private sector.

2. Assistant Area Commander–Logistics

The Area Command Logistics Chief provides facilities, services, and materials at the Area Command level and ensures the effective allocation of critical resources and supplies among the IMTs.

3. Assistant Area Commander–Planning

The Area Command Planning Chief collects information from various IMTs to assess and evaluate potential conflicts in establishing incident objectives, strategies, and priorities for allocating critical resources.

4. Area Command Aviation Coordinator

An Aviation Coordinator is assigned when aviation resources are competing for common airspace and critical resources, and works in coordination with incident aviation organizations to evaluate potential conflicts, develop common airspace management procedures, ensure aviation safety, and allocate critical resources in accordance with Area Command priorities.

5. Area Command Support Positions

The following Area Command positions are activated as necessary:

- **Resources Unit Leader:** Tracks and maintains the status and availability of critical resources assigned to each incident under the Assistant Area Commander–Planning.
- **Situation Unit Leader:** Monitors the status of objectives for each incident or IMT assigned to the Assistant Area Commander–Planning.
- **Public Information Officer:** Provides coordination between incident locations and serves as the point of contact for media requests to the Area Command.
- **Liaison Officer:** Helps maintain off-incident interagency contacts and coordination.

C. LOCATION

The following guidelines should be followed in locating an Area Command:

- To the extent possible, the Area Command should be established in close proximity to the incidents under its authority. This makes it easier for the Area Commander and the ICs to meet and otherwise interact.

- It is, however, best not to co-locate an Area Command with any individual ICP. Doing so might cause confusion with the Command and Management activities associated with that particular incident.

- Area Commands must establish effective, efficient communications, coordination processes, and protocols with subordinate ICs, as well as with other incident management organizations involved in incident operations.

- The facility used to house the organization should be large enough to accommodate a full Area Command staff. It should also be able to accommodate meetings between the Area Command staff, the ICs, and Agency Administrators/Executives as well as news media representatives.

D. REPORTING RELATIONSHIPS

When an Area Command is involved in coordinating multiple incident management activities, the following reporting relationships will apply:

- The ICs for the incidents under the Area Command's authority report to the Area Commander.

- The Area Commander is accountable to the agency(s) or to the jurisdictional executive(s) or administrator(s).

- If one or more incidents within the Area Command are multijurisdictional, a Unified Area Command should be established.

National Incident Management System

TAB 7—FACILITIES AND LOCATIONS

Several kinds and types of facilities may be established in and around the incident area. The requirements of the incident and the desires of the IC/UC will determine the specific kinds and locations of facilities and may consist of the following designated facilities, among others.

A. INCIDENT COMMAND POST

The ICP signifies the location of the tactical-level, on-scene incident command organization. It typically comprises the Incident Command and the Command and General Staffs, but may include other designated incident personnel from Federal, State, tribal, and local departments and agencies, as well as NGOs and the private sector. Typically, the ICP is located at or in the immediate vicinity of the incident site and is the location for the conduct of direct, on-scene control of tactical operations. Incident planning is conducted at the ICP; an incident communications center also would normally be established at this location. The ICP may be co-located with the Incident Base, if the communications requirements can be met.

B. INCIDENT BASE

An Incident Base is the location at which primary support activities are conducted. A single Incident Base is established to house equipment and personnel support operations. The Incident Base should be designed to be able to support operations at multiple incident sites.

C. CAMPS

Camps are separate from the Incident Base and are located as satellites to the Incident Base, where they can best support incident operations. Camps provide support, such as food, sleeping areas, and sanitation. Camps may also provide minor maintenance and servicing of equipment. Camps may be relocated to meet changing operational requirements.

D. STAGING AREAS

Staging Areas are established for the temporary location of available resources. Staging Areas will be established by the Operations Section Chief to enable positioning of and accounting for resources not immediately assigned. A Staging Area can be any location in which personnel, supplies, and equipment can be temporarily housed or parked while awaiting operational assignment. Staging Areas may include temporary feeding, fueling, and sanitation services. The Operations Section Chief assigns a manager for each Staging Area, who checks in all incoming resources, dispatches resources at the Operations Section Chief's request, and requests Logistics Section support, as necessary, for resources located in the Staging Area.

APPENDIX B: INCIDENT COMMAND SYSTEM

TAB 8—THE PLANNING PROCESS AND THE IAP

A. OVERVIEW

Sound, timely planning provides the foundation for effective incident management. The NIMS planning process described below represents a template for strategic, operational, and tactical planning that includes all steps that an IC/UC and other members of the Command and General Staffs should take to develop and disseminate an IAP. The planning process may begin with the scheduling of a planned event, the identification of a credible threat, or the initial response to an actual or impending event. The process continues with the implementation of the formalized steps and the staffing required to develop a written IAP.

A clear, concise IAP template is essential to guide the initial incident management decision process and the continuing collective planning activities of IMTs. The planning process should provide the following:

- Current information that accurately describes the incident situation and resource status.
- Predictions of the probable course of events.
- Alternative strategies to attain critical incident objectives.
- An accurate, realistic IAP for the next operational period.

Five primary phases should be followed in sequence to ensure a comprehensive IAP. These phases are designed to enable the accomplishment of incident objectives within a specified time. The IAP must provide clear strategic direction and include a comprehensive listing of the tactics, resources, reserves, and support required to accomplish each overarching incident objective. The comprehensive IAP will state the sequence of events for achieving multiple incident objectives in a coordinated way. However, the IAP is a living document that is based on the best available information at the time of the Planning Meeting. Planning Meetings should not be delayed in anticipation of future information.

> The five primary phases in the planning process are to understand the situation; establish incident objectives and strategy; develop the plan; prepare and disseminate the plan; and execute, evaluate, and revise the plan.

The primary phases of the planning process are essentially the same for the IC who develops the initial plan, for the IC and Operations Section Chief revising the initial plan for extended operations, and for the IMT developing a formal IAP. During the initial stages of incident management, planners should develop a simple plan that can be communicated through concise oral briefings. Frequently, this plan must be developed very quickly and with incomplete situation information. As the incident management effort evolves, additional lead time, staff, information systems, and technologies enable more detailed planning and cataloging of events and lessons learned.

The five primary phases in the planning process are:

1. Understand the Situation

The first phase includes gathering, recording, analyzing, and displaying situation, resource, and incident-potential information in a manner that will facilitate:

- Increased situational awareness of the magnitude, complexity, and potential impact of the incident.
- The ability to determine the resources required to develop and implement an effective IAP.

2. Establish Incident Objectives and Strategy

The second phase includes formulating and prioritizing measurable incident objectives and identifying an appropriate strategy. The incident objectives and strategy must conform to the legal obligations and management objectives of all affected agencies, and may need to include specific issues relevant to critical infrastructure.

Reasonable alternative strategies that will accomplish overall incident objectives are identified, analyzed, and evaluated to determine the most appropriate strategy for the situation at hand. Evaluation criteria include public health and safety factors, estimated costs, and various environmental, legal, and political considerations.

3. Develop the Plan

The third phase involves determining the tactical direction and the specific resources, reserves, and support requirements for implementing the selected strategies and tactics for the operational period.

Before the formal Planning Meetings, each member of the Command and General Staffs is responsible for gathering certain information to support the proposed plan.

4. Prepare and Disseminate the Plan

The fourth phase involves preparing the plan in a format that is appropriate for the level of complexity of the incident. For the initial response, the format is a well-prepared outline for an oral briefing. For most incidents that will span multiple operational periods, the plan will be developed in writing according to ICS procedures.

5. Execute, Evaluate, and Revise the Plan

The planning process includes the requirement to execute and evaluate planned activities and check the accuracy of information to be used in planning for subsequent operational periods. The General Staff should regularly compare planned progress with actual progress. When deviations occur and when new information emerges, it should be included in the first step of the process used for modifying the current plan or developing the plan for the subsequent operational period.

B. RESPONSIBILITIES AND SPECIFIC PLANNING ACTIVITIES

1. Operational Period Planning Cycle

Figure B-9 is a graphical representation of the planning cycle.

Figure B-9. Operational Period Planning Cycle

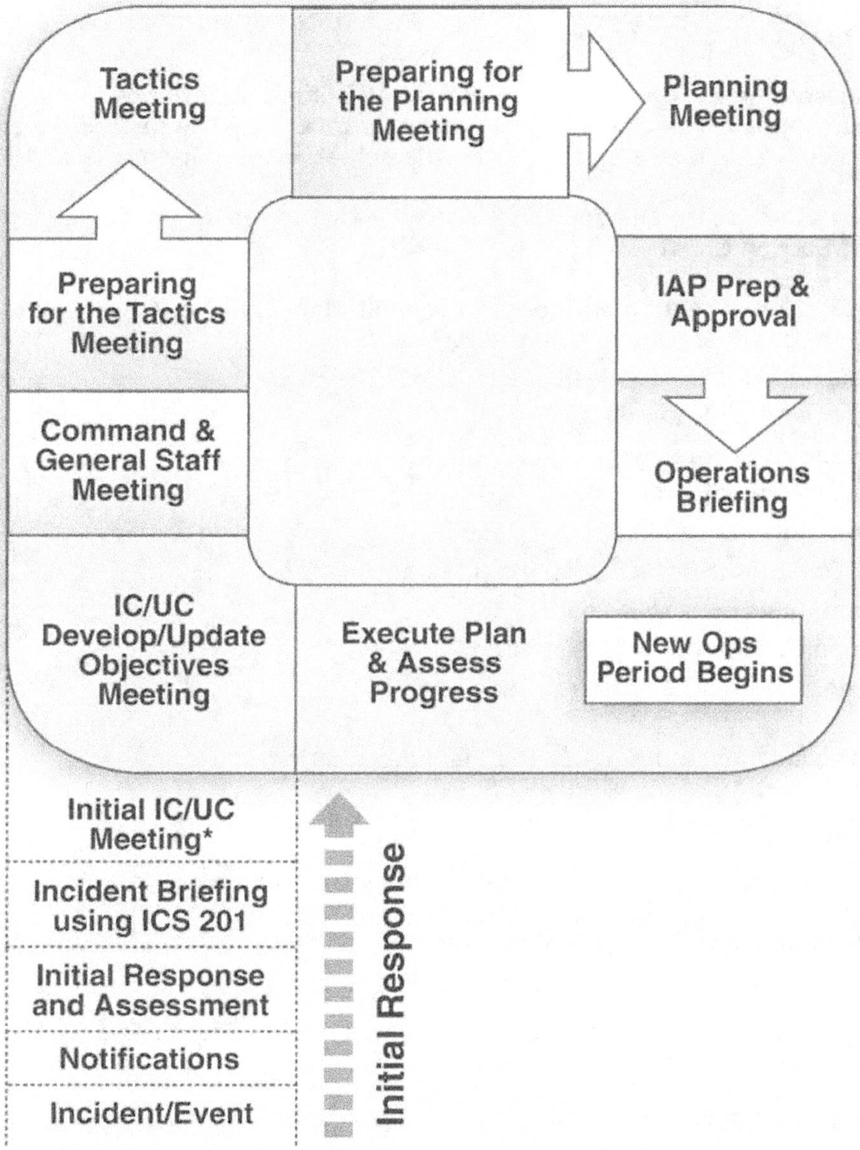

*During this timeframe a meeting with the Agency Administrator/Executive can occur.

2. Planning Steps: Understanding the Situation and Establishing Objectives and Strategy

The Planning Section Chief should take the following actions prior to the initial Planning Meeting (if possible, obtain a completed Incident Briefing (ICS 201)):

- Evaluate the current situation and decide whether the current planning is adequate for the remainder of the operational period (i.e., until the next plan takes effect).

- Advise the IC and the Operations Section Chief of any suggested revisions to the current plan, as necessary.

- Establish a planning cycle for the incident.

- When requested, participate in the Objectives Meeting to contribute to the development/update of incident objectives and strategies. The task of developing incident objectives and strategies is often the sole responsibility of the IC/UC.

- Participate in the Tactics Meeting, if held, to review the tactics developed by the Operations Section Chief.

- Determine Planning Meeting attendees in consultation with the IC. For major incidents, attendees should include the following:
  - Incident Commander.
  - Command Staff members.
  - General Staff members.
  - Resources Unit Leader.
  - Situation Unit Leader.
  - Air Operations Branch Director (if established).
  - Communications Unit Leader.
  - Technical specialists (as required).
  - Agency Representatives (as required).

- Establish the location and time for the Planning Meeting.

- Ensure that planning boards and forms are available.

- Notify necessary support staff about the meeting and their assignments.

- Ensure that a current situation and resource briefing will be available for the meeting.

- Obtain an estimate of resource availability for use in planning for the next operational period.

- Obtain necessary agency policy, legal, or fiscal constraints for use in the Planning Meeting.

3. Conducting the Planning Meeting

The Planning Meeting is normally conducted by the Planning Section Chief. The sequence of steps that follows is intended to aid the Planning Section Chief in developing the IAP. The planning steps are used with the Operational Planning Worksheet (ICS 215).

a. Give a briefing on situation, resource status, and incident potential

The Planning Section Chief and/or Resources and Situation Unit Leaders should provide an up-to-date briefing on the situation. Information for this briefing may come from any or all of the following sources:

- Initial Incident Commander.
- Incident Briefing (ICS 201).
- Field observations.
- Operations reports.
- Regional resources and situation reports.

b. Set/Review established objectives

The IC/UC is responsible for this step. The incident objectives are not limited to any single operational period but will consider the total incident situation. The IC/UC establishes the general strategy to be used, states any major constraints (policy, legal, or fiscal) on accomplishing the objectives, and offers appropriate contingency considerations.

c. Plot operational lines, establish Branch/Division boundaries, and identify Group assignments

This step is normally accomplished by the Operations Section Chief (for the next operational period) in conjunction with the Planning Section Chief, who will establish Division and Branch boundaries for geographical Divisions and determine the need for functional Group assignments for the next operational period. The operational boundaries will be plotted on the map.

d. Specify tactics for each Division/Group

After determining Division geographical assignments or Group functions, the Operations Section Chief will establish the specific work assignments to be performed for the next operational period. Tactics (work assignments) should be specific and within the boundaries set by the IC/UC general objectives and established strategies. These work assignments should be recorded on the Operational Planning Worksheet (ICS 215). At this time, the IC/UC, Operations Section Chief, and Planning Section Chief should also consider the need for any alternative strategies or tactics and ensure that these are properly noted on the Operational Planning Worksheet .

e. Specify resources needed by Division/Group

After specifying tactics for each Division/Group, the Operations Section Chief, in conjunction with the Planning Section Chief, will determine the resource needs to accomplish the work assignments. Resource needs will be recorded on the Operational Planning Worksheet (ICS

215). Resource needs should be considered on the basis of the type of resources required to accomplish the assignment.

f. Specify operations facilities and reporting locations and plot on map

The Operations Section Chief, in conjunction with the Planning and Logistics Section Chiefs, should designate and make available the facilities and reporting locations required to accomplish Operations Section work assignments. The Operations Section Chief should indicate the reporting time requirements for the resources and any special resource assignments.

g. Develop resource order

The Planning Section Chief should assess resource needs based on the needs indicated by the Operations Section Chief and resources data available from the Resources Unit. The Operational Planning Worksheet (ICS 215), when properly completed, will show resource requirements and the resources available to meet those requirements. Subtracting the resources available from those required will indicate any additional resource needs. From this assessment, a new resource order can be developed and provided to the IC/UC for approval and then placed through normal dispatch channels by the Logistics Section.

h. Consider Communications, Medical, and Traffic Plan requirements

The IAP will normally consist of the Incident Objectives (ICS 202), Organization Chart (ICS 203), Assignment List (ICS 204), and a map of the incident area. Larger incidents may require additional supporting attachments, such as a separate Incident Radio Communications Plan (ICS 205), a Medical Plan (ICS 206), and possibly a Traffic Plan. The Planning Section Chief should determine the need for these attachments and ensure that the appropriate Units prepare them. The IAP and attachments will normally include the items listed in Table B-2.

Table B-2. The IAP and Typical Attachments

Component	Normally Prepared By
Incident Objectives (ICS 202)	Incident Commander
Organization Assignment List or Chart (ICS 203)	Resources Unit
Assignment List (ICS 204)	Resources Unit
Incident Radio Communications Plan (ICS 205)	Communications Unit
Medical Plan (ICS 206)	Medical Unit
Incident Maps	Situation Unit
Safety Message Plan (ICS 208)	Safety Officer

Other Potential Components (incident dependent)	
Air Operations Summary (ICS 220)	Air Operations
Traffic Plan	Ground Support Unit
Decontamination Plan	Technical Specialist
Waste Management or Disposal Plan	Technical Specialist
Demobilization Checkout (ICS 221)	Demobilization Unit
Site Security Plan	Law Enforcement, Technical Specialist, or Security Manager
Investigative Plan	Law Enforcement
Evidence Recovery Plan	Law Enforcement
Evacuation Plan	As required
Sheltering/Mass Care Plan	As required
Other (as required)	As required

i. Finalize, approve, and implement the Incident Action Plan

The Planning Section, in conjunction with the Operations Section, is responsible for seeing that the IAP is completed, reviewed, and distributed. The following is the sequence of steps for accomplishing this:

- Set the deadline for completing IAP attachments (see Table B-3).
- Obtain plan attachments and review them for completeness and approvals. Before completing the plan, the Planning Section Chief should review the Division and Group tactical work assignments for any changes due to lack of resource availability. The Resources Unit may then transfer Division/Group assignment information, including alternatives from the Operational Planning Worksheet (ICS 215), onto the Division Assignment Lists (ICS 204).
- Determine the number of IAPs required.
- Arrange with the Documentation Unit to reproduce the IAP.
- Review the IAP to ensure it is up to date and complete prior to the operations briefing and plan distribution.
- Provide the IAP briefing plan, as required, and distribute the plan prior to beginning of the new operational period.

Table B-3. ICS Forms That Can Aid the Planning Process*

Number	Purpose
ICS 201 (p.1)**	Incident Briefing Map
ICS 201 (p.2)**	Summary of Current Actions
ICS 201 (p.3)**	Current Organization
ICS 201 (p.4)**	Resources Summary
ICS 202	Incident Objectives
ICS 203	Organization Assignment List
ICS 204	Assignment List
ICS 205	Incident Radio Communications Plan
ICS 206	Medical Plan
ICS 207	Incident Organization Chart (wall mounted)
ICS 209	Incident Status Summary
ICS 210	Status Change
ICS 211	Incident Check-In List
ICS 213	General Message
ICS 215	Operational Planning Worksheet
ICS 215A	Hazard Risk Analysis

*ICS Forms are guidance documents to assist in writing an agency's IAP. Some modification to the forms can be made to suit an agency's need more effectively, as long as the nature of each form or numbering is not altered.

**The ICS 201 Forms are the initial summary forms provided at the start of an incident. The information they provide can help craft an IAP, but the ICS 201 Forms may not be included in the formal written IAP.

TAB 9—ICS FORMS

This section describes some common ICS Forms. The individual forms may be tailored to meet an agency's needs. More importantly, even though the format is flexible, the form number and purpose of the specific type of form (e.g., Assignment List (ICS 204) defines the assignments for a Division or Group) must remain intact in order to maintain consistency and facilitate immediate identification and interoperability, and for ease of use.

A. ICS FORMS

The following provides brief descriptions of selected ICS Forms. This list is not all inclusive; other forms are available online, commercially, and in a variety of formats.

1. ICS 201 – Incident Briefing

Most often used by the initial IC, this four-section document (often produced as four pages) allows for the capture of vital incident information prior to the implementation of the formal planning process. ICS 201 allows for a concise and complete transition of command briefing to an incoming new IC. In addition, this form may serve as the full extent of incident command and control documentation if the situation is resolved by the initial response resources and organization. This form is designed to be transferred easily to the members of the Command and General Staffs as they arrive and begin work. It is not included as a part of the formal written IAP.

2. ICS 202 – Incident Objectives

ICS 202 serves as the first page of a written IAP. It includes incident information, a listing of the IC's objectives for the operational period, pertinent weather information, a general safety message, and a table of contents for the plan. Signature blocks are provided.

3. ICS 203 – Organization Assignment List

ICS 203 is typically the second page of the IAP. It provides a full accounting of incident management and supervisory staff for that operational period.

4. ICS 204 – Assignment List

ICS 204 is included in multiples, based on the organizational structure of the Operations Section for the operational period. Each Division/Group will have its own page, listing the Supervisor for the Division/Group (including Branch Director if assigned) and the specific assigned resources with leader name and number of personnel assigned to each resource. This document then describes in detail the specific actions the Division or Group will be taking in support of the overall incident objectives. Any special instructions will be included as well as the elements of the Incident Radio Communications Plan (ICS 205) that apply to that Division or Group.

5. ICS 205 – Incident Radio Communications Plan

ICS 205 is used to provide information on all radio frequency assignments down to the Division/Group level.

6. ICS 206 – Medical Plan

ICS 206 presents the incident's Medical Plan to care for responder medical emergencies.

7. ICS 209 – Incident Status Summary

ICS 209 collects basic incident decision support information and is the primary mechanism for reporting this situational information to incident coordination and support organizations and the Agency Administrators/Executives.

8. ICS 211 – Incident Check-In List

ICS 211 documents the check-in process. Check-in recorders report check-in information to the Resources Unit.

9. ICS 215 – Operational Planning Worksheet

ICS 215 is used in the incident Planning Meeting to develop tactical assignments and resources needed to achieve incident objectives and strategies.

10. ICS 215A – Hazard Risk Analysis

ICS 215A communicates to the Operations and Planning Section Chiefs the safety and health issues identified by the Safety Officer. The ICS 215A form identifies mitigation measures to address the identified safety issues.

TAB 10—SUMMARY OF MAJOR ICS POSITIONS

This section lists the primary functions of each major ICS position.

Table B-4. Summary Table of Major ICS Positions*

Major ICS Position	Primary Functions
Incident Commander or Unified Command	• Have clear authority and know agency policy. • Ensure incident safety. • Establish the ICP. • Set priorities, and determine incident objectives and strategies to be followed. • Establish ICS organization needed to manage the incident. • Approve the IAP. • Coordinate Command and General Staff activities. • Approve resource requests and use of volunteers and auxiliary personnel. • Order demobilization as needed. • Ensure after-action reports are completed. • Authorize information release to the media.
Public Information Officer	• Determine, according to direction from IC, any limits on information release. • Develop accurate, accessible, and timely information for use in press/media briefings. • Obtain the IC's approval of news releases. • Conduct periodic media briefings. • Arrange for tours and other interviews or briefings that may be required. • Monitor and forward media information that may be useful to incident planning. • Maintain current information summaries and/or displays on the incident. • Make information about the incident available to incident personnel. • Participate in Planning Meetings. • Implement methods to monitor rumor control.

*The Intelligence/Investigations Function may be under the direction of a separate General Staff position.

Major ICS Position	Primary Functions
Safety Officer	• Identify and mitigate hazardous situations. • Create a Safety Plan. • Ensure safety messages and briefings are made. • Exercise emergency authority to stop and prevent unsafe acts . • Review the IAP for safety implications. • Assign assistants qualified to evaluate special hazards. • Initiate preliminary investigation of accidents within the incident area. • Review and approve the Medical Plan. • Participate in Planning Meetings to address anticipated hazards associated with future operations.
Liaison Officer	• Act as a point of contact for Agency Representatives. • Maintain a list of assisting and cooperating agencies and Agency Representatives. • Assist in setting up and coordinating interagency contacts. • Monitor incident operations to identify current or potential interorganizational problems. • Participate in Planning Meetings, providing current resource status, including limitations and capabilities of agency resources. • Provide agency-specific demobilization information and requirements.
Operations Section Chief	• Ensure safety of tactical operations. • Manage tactical operations. • Develop operations portions of the IAP. • Supervise execution of operations portions of the IAP. • Request additional resources to support tactical operations. • Approve release of resources from active operational assignments. • Make or approve expedient changes to the IAP. • Maintain close contact with the IC, subordinate Operations personnel, and other agencies involved in the incident.

Major ICS Position	Primary Functions
Planning Section Chief	• Collect and manage all incident-relevant operational data. • Supervise preparation of the IAP. • Provide input to the IC and Operations in preparing the IAP. • Incorporate Traffic, Medical, and Communications Plans and other supporting material into the IAP. • Conduct/facilitate Planning Meetings. • Reassign out-of-service personnel within the ICS organization already on scene, as appropriate. • Compile and display incident status information. • Establish information requirements and reporting schedules for Units (e.g., Resources Unit, Situation Unit). • Determine need for specialized resources. • Assemble and disassemble Task Forces and Strike Teams not assigned to Operations. • Establish specialized data collection systems as necessary (e.g., weather). • Assemble information on alternative strategies. • Provide periodic predictions on incident potential. • Report significant changes in incident status. • Oversee preparation of the Demobilization Plan.
Logistics Section Chief	• Provide all facilities, transportation, communications, supplies, equipment maintenance and fueling, food, and medical services for incident personnel, and all off-incident resources. • Manage all incident logistics. • Provide logistics input to the IAP. • Brief Logistics staff as needed. • Identify anticipated and known incident service and support requirements. • Request additional resources as needed. • Ensure and oversee development of Traffic, Medical, and Communications Plans as required. • Oversee demobilization of Logistics Section and associated resources.

Major ICS Position	Primary Functions
Finance/Administration Section Chief	• Manage all financial aspects of an incident. • Provide financial and cost analysis information as requested. • Ensure compensation and claims functions are being addressed relative to the incident. • Gather pertinent information from briefings with responsible agencies. • Develop an operational plan for the Finance/Administration Section and fill Section supply and support needs. • Determine the need to set up and operate an incident commissary. • Meet with assisting and cooperating Agency Representatives as needed. • Maintain daily contact with agency(s) headquarters on finance matters. • Ensure that personnel time records are completed accurately and transmitted to home agencies. • Ensure that all obligation documents initiated at the incident are properly prepared and completed. • Brief agency administrative personnel on all incident-related financial issues needing attention or followup. • Provide input to the IAP.

GLOSSARY OF KEY TERMS

For the purposes of NIMS, the following terms and definitions apply:

Accessible: Having the legally required features and/or qualities that ensure easy entrance, participation, and usability of places, programs, services, and activities by individuals with a wide variety of disabilities.

Acquisition Procedures: A process used to obtain resources to support operational requirements.

Agency: A division of government with a specific function offering a particular kind of assistance. In the Incident Command System, agencies are defined either as jurisdictional (having statutory responsibility for incident management) or as assisting or cooperating (providing resources or other assistance). Governmental organizations are most often in charge of an incident, though in certain circumstances private-sector organizations may be included. Additionally, nongovernmental organizations may be included to provide support.

Agency Administrator/Executive: The official responsible for administering policy for an agency or jurisdiction. An Agency Administrator/Executive (or other public official with jurisdictional responsibility for the incident) usually makes the decision to establish an Area Command.

Agency Dispatch: The agency or jurisdictional facility from which resources are sent to incidents.

Agency Representative: A person assigned by a primary, assisting, or cooperating Federal, State, tribal, or local government agency, or nongovernmental or private organization, that has been delegated authority to make decisions affecting that agency's or organization's participation in incident management activities following appropriate consultation with the leadership of that agency.

All-Hazards: Describing an incident, natural or manmade, that warrants action to protect life, property, environment, and public health or safety, and to minimize disruptions of government, social, or economic activities.

Allocated Resource: Resource dispatched to an incident.

Area Command: An organization established to oversee the management of multiple incidents that are each being handled by a separate Incident Command System organization or to oversee the management of a very large or evolving incident that has multiple Incident Management Teams engaged. An Agency Administrator/Executive or other public official with jurisdictional responsibility for the incident usually makes the decision to establish an Area Command. An Area Command is activated only if necessary, depending on the complexity of the incident and incident management span-of-control considerations.

Assessment: The process of acquiring, collecting, processing, examining, analyzing, evaluating, monitoring, and interpreting the data, information, evidence, objects, measurements, images, sound, etc., whether tangible or intangible, to provide a basis for decisionmaking.

Assigned Resource: Resource checked in and assigned work tasks on an incident.

Assignment: Task given to a personnel resource to perform within a given operational period that is based on operational objectives defined in the Incident Action Plan.

Assistant: Title for subordinates of principal Command Staff positions. The title indicates a level of technical capability, qualifications, and responsibility subordinate to the primary positions. Assistants may also be assigned to Unit Leaders.

Assisting Agency: An agency or organization providing personnel, services, or other resources to the agency with direct responsibility for incident management. See **Supporting Agency**.

Available Resource: Resource assigned to an incident, checked in, and available for a mission assignment, normally located in a Staging Area.

Badging: The assignment of physical incident-specific credentials to establish legitimacy and limit access to various incident sites.

Branch: The organizational level having functional or geographical responsibility for major aspects of incident operations. A Branch is organizationally situated between the Section Chief and the Division or Group in the Operations Section, and between the Section and Units in the Logistics Section. Branches are identified by the use of Roman numerals or by functional area.

Cache: A predetermined complement of tools, equipment, and/or supplies stored in a designated location, available for incident use.

Camp: A geographical site within the general incident area (separate from the Incident Base) that is equipped and staffed to provide sleeping, food, water, and sanitary services to incident personnel.

Categorizing Resources: The process of organizing resources by category, kind, and type, including size, capacity, capability, skill, and other characteristics. This makes the resource ordering and dispatch process within and across organizations and agencies, and between governmental and nongovernmental entities, more efficient, and ensures that the resources received are appropriate to their needs.

Certifying Personnel: The process of authoritatively attesting that individuals meet professional standards for the training, experience, and performance required for key incident management functions.

Chain of Command: The orderly line of authority within the ranks of the incident management organization.

Check-In: The process through which resources first report to an incident. All responders, regardless of agency affiliation, must report in to receive an assignment in accordance with the procedures established by the Incident Commander.

Chief: The Incident Command System title for individuals responsible for management of functional Sections: Operations, Planning, Logistics, Finance/Administration, and Intelligence/Investigations (if established as a separate Section).

Command: The act of directing, ordering, or controlling by virtue of explicit statutory, regulatory, or delegated authority.

Command Staff: The staff who report directly to the Incident Commander, including the Public Information Officer, Safety Officer, Liaison Officer, and other positions as required. They may have an assistant or assistants, as needed.

Common Operating Picture: An overview of an incident by all relevant parties that provides incident information enabling the Incident Commander/Unified Command and any supporting agencies and organizations to make effective, consistent, and timely decisions.

Common Terminology: Normally used words and phrases—avoiding the use of different words/phrases for same concepts—to ensure consistency and to allow diverse incident management and support organizations to work together across a wide variety of incident management functions and hazard scenarios.

Communications: The process of transmission of information through verbal, written, or symbolic means.

Communications/Dispatch Center: Agency or interagency dispatch centers, 911 call centers, emergency control or command dispatch centers, or any naming convention given to the facility and staff that handles emergency calls from the public and communication with emergency management/response personnel. The center can serve as a primary coordination and support element of the Multiagency Coordination System(s) (MACS) for an incident until other elements of the MACS are formally established.

Complex: Two or more individual incidents located in the same general area and assigned to a single Incident Commander or to Unified Command.

Comprehensive Preparedness Guide 101: A guide designed to assist jurisdictions with developing operations plans. It promotes a common understanding of the fundamentals of planning and decisionmaking to help emergency planners examine a hazard and produce integrated, coordinated, and synchronized plans.

Continuity of Government: A coordinated effort within the Federal Government's executive branch to ensure that National Essential Functions continue to be performed during a catastrophic emergency (as defined in National Security Presidential Directive 51/Homeland Security Presidential Directive 20).

Continuity of Operations: An effort within individual organizations to ensure that Primary Mission Essential Functions continue to be performed during a wide range of emergencies.

Cooperating Agency: An agency supplying assistance other than direct operational or support functions or resources to the incident management effort.

Coordinate: To advance an analysis and exchange of information systematically among principals who have or may have a need to know certain information to carry out specific incident management responsibilities.

Corrective Actions: The implementation of procedures that are based on lessons learned from actual incidents or from training and exercises.

Credentialing: The authentication and verification of the certification and identity of designated incident managers and emergency responders.

Critical Infrastructure: Assets, systems, and networks, whether physical or virtual, so vital to the United States that the incapacitation or destruction of such assets, systems, or networks would have a debilitating impact on security, national economic security, national public health or safety, or any combination of those matters.

Delegation of Authority: A statement provided to the Incident Commander by the Agency Executive delegating authority and assigning responsibility. The delegation of authority can include objectives, priorities, expectations, constraints, and other considerations or guidelines, as needed. Many agencies require written delegation of authority to be given to the Incident Commander prior to assuming command on larger incidents. (Also known as **Letter of Expectation.**)

Demobilization: The orderly, safe, and efficient return of an incident resource to its original location and status.

Department Operations Center (DOC): An Emergency Operations Center (EOC) specific to a single department or agency. The focus of a DOC is on internal agency incident management and response. DOCs are often linked to and, in most cases, are physically represented in a combined agency EOC by authorized agent(s) for the department or agency.

Deputy: A fully qualified individual who, in the absence of a superior, can be delegated the authority to manage a functional operation or to perform a specific task. In some cases a deputy can act as relief for a superior, and therefore must be fully qualified in the position. Deputies generally can be assigned to the Incident Commander, General Staff, and Branch Directors.

Director: The Incident Command System title for individuals responsible for supervision of a Branch.

Dispatch: The ordered movement of a resource or resources to an assigned operational mission, or an administrative move from one location to another.

Division: The organizational level having responsibility for operations within a defined geographic area. Divisions are established when the number of resources exceeds the manageable span of control of the Section Chief. See **Group.**

Emergency: Any incident, whether natural or manmade, that requires responsive action to protect life or property. Under the Robert T. Stafford Disaster Relief and Emergency Assistance Act, an emergency means any occasion or instance for which, in the determination of the President, Federal assistance is needed to supplement State and local efforts and capabilities to save lives and to protect property and public health and safety, or to lessen or avert the threat of a catastrophe in any part of the United States.

Emergency Management Assistance Compact (EMAC): A congressionally ratified organization that provides form and structure to interstate mutual aid. Through EMAC, a disaster-affected State can request and receive assistance from other member States quickly and efficiently, resolving two key issues up front: liability and reimbursement.

Emergency Management/Response Personnel: Includes Federal, State, territorial, tribal, substate regional, and local governments, NGOs, private sector-organizations, critical infrastructure owners and operators, and all other organizations and individuals who assume an emergency management role. (Also known as emergency responder.)

Emergency Operations Center (EOC): The physical location at which the coordination of information and resources to support incident management (on-scene operations) activities normally takes place. An EOC may be a temporary facility or may be located in a more central or permanently established facility, perhaps at a higher level of organization within a jurisdiction. EOCs may be organized by major functional disciplines (e.g., fire, law enforcement, medical services), by jurisdiction (e.g., Federal, State, regional, tribal, city, county), or by some combination thereof.

Emergency Operations Plan: An ongoing plan for responding to a wide variety of potential hazards.

Emergency Public Information: Information that is disseminated primarily in anticipation of or during an emergency. In addition to providing situational information to the public, it frequently provides directive actions required to be taken by the general public.

Evacuation: The organized, phased, and supervised withdrawal, dispersal, or removal of civilians from dangerous or potentially dangerous areas, and their reception and care in safe areas.

Event: See Planned Event.

Federal: Of or pertaining to the Federal Government of the United States of America.

Field Operations Guide: Durable pocket or desk guides that contain essential information required to perform specific assignments or functions.

Finance/Administration Section: The Incident Command System Section responsible for all administrative and financial considerations surrounding an incident.

Function: One of the five major activities in the Incident Command System: Command, Operations, Planning, Logistics, and Finance/Administration. A sixth function, Intelligence/Investigations, may be established, if required, to meet incident management needs. The term *function* is also used when describing the activity involved (e.g., the planning function).

General Staff: A group of incident management personnel organized according to function and reporting to the Incident Commander. The General Staff normally consists of the Operations Section Chief, Planning Section Chief, Logistics Section Chief, and Finance/Administration Section Chief. An Intelligence/Investigations Chief may be established, if required, to meet incident management needs.

Group: An organizational subdivision established to divide the incident management structure into functional areas of operation. Groups are composed of resources assembled to perform a special function not necessarily within a single geographic division. See **Division.**

Hazard: Something that is potentially dangerous or harmful, often the root cause of an unwanted outcome.

Incident: An occurrence, natural or manmade, that requires a response to protect life or property. Incidents can, for example, include major disasters, emergencies, terrorist attacks, terrorist threats, civil unrest, wildland and urban fires, floods, hazardous materials spills, nuclear accidents, aircraft accidents, earthquakes, hurricanes, tornadoes, tropical storms, tsunamis, war-related disasters, public health and medical emergencies, and other occurrences requiring an emergency response.

Incident Action Plan: An oral or written plan containing general objectives reflecting the overall strategy for managing an incident. It may include the identification of operational resources and assignments. It may also include attachments that provide direction and important information for management of the incident during one or more operational periods.

Incident Base: The location at which primary Logistics functions for an incident are coordinated and administered. There is only one Base per incident. (Incident name or other designator will be added to the term Base.) The Incident Command Post may be co-located with the Incident Base.

Incident Command: The Incident Command System organizational element responsible for overall management of the incident and consisting of the Incident Commander (either single or unified command structure) and any assigned supporting staff.

Incident Commander (IC): The individual responsible for all incident activities, including the development of strategies and tactics and the ordering and release of resources. The IC has overall authority and responsibility for conducting incident operations and is responsible for the management of all incident operations at the incident site.

Incident Command Post (ICP): The field location where the primary functions are performed. The ICP may be co-located with the Incident Base or other incident facilities.

Incident Command System (ICS): A standardized on-scene emergency management construct specifically designed to provide an integrated organizational structure that reflects the complexity and demands of single or multiple incidents, without being hindered by jurisdictional boundaries. ICS is the combination of facilities, equipment, personnel, procedures, and communications operating within a common organizational structure, designed to aid in the management of resources during incidents. It is used for all kinds of emergencies and is applicable to small as well as large and complex incidents. ICS is used by various jurisdictions and functional agencies, both public and private, to organize field-level incident management operations.

Incident Management: The broad spectrum of activities and organizations providing effective and efficient operations, coordination, and support applied at all levels of government, utilizing both governmental and nongovernmental resources to plan for, respond to, and recover from an incident, regardless of cause, size, or complexity.

Incident Management Team (IMT): An Incident Commander and the appropriate Command and General Staff personnel assigned to an incident. The level of training and experience of the IMT members, coupled with the identified formal response requirements and responsibilities of the IMT, are factors in determining "type," or level, of IMT.

Incident Objectives: Statements of guidance and direction needed to select appropriate strategy(s) and the tactical direction of resources. Incident objectives are based on realistic expectations of what can be accomplished when all allocated resources have been effectively deployed. Incident objectives must be achievable and measurable, yet flexible enough to allow strategic and tactical alternatives.

Information Management: The collection, organization, and control over the structure, processing, and delivery of information from one or more sources and distribution to one or more audiences who have a stake in that information.

Integrated Planning System: A system designed to provide common processes for developing and integrating plans for the Federal Government to establish a comprehensive approach to national planning in accordance with the Homeland Security Management System as outlined in the *National Strategy for Homeland Security*.

Intelligence/Investigations: An organizational subset within ICS. Intelligence gathered within the Intelligence/Investigations function is information that either leads to the detection, prevention, apprehension, and prosecution of criminal activities—or the individual(s) involved—including terrorist incidents or information that leads to determination of the cause of a given incident (regardless of the source) such as public health events or fires with unknown origins. This is different from the normal operational and situational intelligence gathered and reported by the Planning Section.

Interoperability: Ability of systems, personnel, and equipment to provide and receive functionality, data, information and/or services to and from other systems, personnel, and equipment, between both public and private agencies, departments, and other organizations, in a manner enabling them to operate effectively together. Allows emergency management/response personnel and their affiliated organizations to communicate within and across agencies and jurisdictions via voice, data, or video-on-demand, in real time, when needed, and when authorized.

Job Aid: Checklist or other visual aid intended to ensure that specific steps of completing a task or assignment are accomplished.

Joint Field Office (JFO): The primary Federal incident management field structure. The JFO is a temporary Federal facility that provides a central location for the coordination of Federal, State, tribal, and local governments and private-sector and nongovernmental organizations with primary responsibility for response and recovery. The JFO structure is organized, staffed, and managed in a manner consistent with *National Incident Management System* principles. Although the JFO uses an Incident Command System structure, the JFO does not manage on-scene operations. Instead, the JFO focuses on providing support to on-scene efforts and conducting broader support operations that may extend beyond the incident site.

Joint Information Center (JIC): A facility established to coordinate all incident-related public information activities. It is the central point of contact for all news media. Public information officials from all participating agencies should co-locate at the JIC.

Joint Information System (JIS): A structure that integrates incident information and public affairs into a cohesive organization designed to provide consistent, coordinated, accurate, accessible, timely, and complete information during crisis or incident operations. The mission of the JIS is to provide a structure and system for developing and delivering coordinated interagency messages; developing, recommending, and executing public information plans and strategies on behalf of the Incident Commander (IC); advising the IC concerning public affairs issues that could affect a response effort; and controlling rumors and inaccurate information that could undermine public confidence in the emergency response effort.

Jurisdiction: A range or sphere of authority. Public agencies have jurisdiction at an incident related to their legal responsibilities and authority. Jurisdictional authority at an incident can be political or geographical (e.g., Federal, State, tribal, local boundary lines) or functional (e.g., law enforcement, public health).

Jurisdictional Agency: The agency having jurisdiction and responsibility for a specific geographical area, or a mandated function.

Key Resource: Any publicly or privately controlled resource essential to the minimal operations of the economy and government.

Letter of Expectation: See **Delegation of Authority**.

Liaison: A form of communication for establishing and maintaining mutual understanding and cooperation.

Liaison Officer: A member of the Command Staff responsible for coordinating with representatives from cooperating and assisting agencies or organizations.

Local Government: Public entities responsible for the security and welfare of a designated area as established by law. A county, municipality, city, town, township, local public authority, school district, special district, intrastate district, council of governments (regardless of whether the council of governments is incorporated as a nonprofit corporation under State law), regional or interstate government entity, or agency or instrumentality of a local government; an Indian tribe or authorized tribal entity, or in Alaska a Native Village or Alaska Regional Native Corporation; a rural community, unincorporated town or village, or other public entity. See Section 2 (10), Homeland Security Act of 2002, Pub. L. 107-296, 116 Stat. 2135 (2002).

Logistics: The process and procedure for providing resources and other services to support incident management.

Logistics Section: The Incident Command System Section responsible for providing facilities, services, and material support for the incident.

Management by Objectives: A management approach that involves a five-step process for achieving the incident goal. The Management by Objectives approach includes the following: establishing overarching incident objectives; developing strategies based on overarching incident objectives; developing and issuing assignments, plans, procedures, and protocols; establishing specific, measurable tactics or tasks for various incident-management functional activities and directing efforts to attain them, in support of defined strategies; and documenting results to measure performance and facilitate corrective action.

Manager: Individual within an Incident Command System organizational unit who is assigned specific managerial responsibilities (e.g., Staging Area Manager or Camp Manager).

Mitigation: Activities providing a critical foundation in the effort to reduce the loss of life and property from natural and/or manmade disasters by avoiding or lessening the impact of a disaster and providing value to the public by creating safer communities. Mitigation seeks to fix the cycle of disaster damage, reconstruction, and repeated damage. These activities or actions, in most cases, will have a long-term sustained effect.

Mobilization: The process and procedures used by all organizations—Federal, State, tribal, and local—for activating, assembling, and transporting all resources that have been requested to respond to or support an incident.

Mobilization Guide: Reference document used by organizations outlining agreements, processes, and procedures used by all participating agencies/organizations for activating, assembling, and transporting resources.

Multiagency Coordination (MAC) Group: A group of administrators or executives, or their appointed representatives, who are typically authorized to commit agency resources and funds. A MAC Group can provide coordinated decisionmaking and resource allocation among cooperating agencies, and may establish the priorities among incidents, harmonize agency policies, and provide strategic guidance and direction to support incident management activities. MAC Groups may also be known as multiagency committees, emergency management committees, or as otherwise defined by the Multiagency Coordination System.

Multiagency Coordination System (MACS): A system that provides the architecture to support coordination for incident prioritization, critical resource allocation, communications systems integration, and information coordination. MACS assist agencies and organizations responding to an incident. The elements of a MACS include facilities, equipment, personnel, procedures, and communications. Two of the most commonly used elements are Emergency Operations Centers and MAC Groups.

Multijurisdictional Incident: An incident requiring action from multiple agencies that each have jurisdiction to manage certain aspects of an incident. In the Incident Command System, these incidents will be managed under a Unified Command.

Mutual Aid Agreement or Assistance Agreement: Written or oral agreement between and among agencies/organizations and/or jurisdictions that provides a mechanism to quickly obtain emergency assistance in the form of personnel, equipment, materials, and other associated services. The primary objective is to facilitate rapid, short-term deployment of emergency support prior to, during, and/or after an incident.

National: Of a nationwide character, including the Federal, State, tribal, and local aspects of governance and policy.

National Essential Functions: A subset of government functions that are necessary to lead and sustain the Nation during a catastrophic emergency and that, therefore, must be supported through continuity of operations and continuity of government capabilities.

National Incident Management System: A set of principles that provides a systematic, proactive approach guiding government agencies at all levels, nongovernmental organizations, and the private sector to work seamlessly to prevent, protect against, respond to, recover from, and mitigate the effects of incidents, regardless of cause, size, location, or complexity, in order to reduce the loss of life or property and harm to the environment.

National Response Framework: A guide to how the Nation conducts all-hazards response.

Nongovernmental Organization (NGO): An entity with an association that is based on interests of its members, individuals, or institutions. It is not created by a government, but it may work cooperatively with government. Such organizations serve a public purpose, not a private benefit. Examples of NGOs include faith-based charity organizations and the American Red Cross. NGOs, including voluntary and faith-based groups, provide relief services to sustain life, reduce physical and emotional distress, and promote the recovery of disaster victims. Often these groups provide specialized services that help individuals with disabilities. NGOs and voluntary organizations play a major role in assisting emergency managers before, during, and after an emergency.

Officer: The Incident Command System title for a person responsible for one of the Command Staff positions of Safety, Liaison, and Public Information.

Operational Period: The time scheduled for executing a given set of operation actions, as specified in the Incident Action Plan. Operational periods can be of various lengths, although usually they last 12 to 24 hours.

Operations Section: The Incident Command System (ICS) Section responsible for all tactical incident operations and implementation of the Incident Action Plan. In ICS, the Operations Section normally includes subordinate Branches, Divisions, and/or Groups.

Organization: Any association or group of persons with like objectives. Examples include, but are not limited to, governmental departments and agencies, nongovernmental organizations, and the private sector.

Personal Responsibility: The obligation to be accountable for one's actions.

Personnel Accountability: The ability to account for the location and welfare of incident personnel. It is accomplished when supervisors ensure that Incident Command System principles and processes are functional and that personnel are working within established incident management guidelines.

Plain Language: Communication that can be understood by the intended audience and meets the purpose of the communicator. For the purpose of the *National Incident Management System*, plain language is designed to eliminate or limit the use of codes and acronyms, as appropriate, during incident response involving more than a single agency.

Planned Event: A scheduled nonemergency activity (e.g., sporting event, concert, parade, etc.).

Planning Meeting: A meeting held as needed before and throughout the duration of an incident to select specific strategies and tactics for incident control operations and for service and support planning. For larger incidents, the Planning Meeting is a major element in the development of the Incident Action Plan.

Planning Section: The Incident Command System Section responsible for the collection, evaluation, and dissemination of operational information related to the incident, and for the preparation and documentation of the Incident Action Plan. This Section also maintains information on the current and forecasted situation and on the status of resources assigned to the incident.

Portability: An approach that facilitates the interaction of systems that are normally distinct. Portability of radio technologies, protocols, and frequencies among emergency management/response personnel will allow for the successful and efficient integration, transport, and deployment of communications systems when necessary. Portability includes the standardized assignment of radio channels across jurisdictions, which allows responders to participate in an incident outside their jurisdiction and still use familiar equipment.

Pre-Positioned Resource: A resource moved to an area near the expected incident site in response to anticipated resource needs.

Preparedness: A continuous cycle of planning, organizing, training, equipping, exercising, evaluating, and taking corrective action in an effort to ensure effective coordination during incident response. Within the *National Incident Management System*, preparedness focuses on the following elements: planning; procedures and protocols; training and exercises; personnel qualification and certification; and equipment certification.

Preparedness Organization: An organization that provides coordination for emergency management and incident response activities before a potential incident. These organizations range from groups of individuals to small committees to large standing organizations that represent a wide variety of committees, planning groups, and other organizations (e.g., Citizen Corps, Local Emergency Planning Committees, Critical Infrastructure Sector Coordinating Councils).

Prevention: Actions to avoid an incident or to intervene to stop an incident from occurring. Prevention involves actions to protect lives and property. It involves applying intelligence and other information to a range of activities that may include such countermeasures as deterrence operations; heightened inspections; improved surveillance and security operations; investigations to determine the full nature and source of the threat; public health and agricultural surveillance and testing processes; immunizations, isolation, or quarantine; and, as appropriate, specific law enforcement operations aimed at deterring, preempting, interdicting, or disrupting illegal activity and apprehending potential perpetrators and bringing them to justice.

Primary Mission Essential Functions: Government functions that must be performed in order to support or implement the performance of National Essential Functions before, during, and in the aftermath of an emergency.

Private Sector: Organizations and individuals that are not part of any governmental structure. The private sector includes for-profit and not-for-profit organizations, formal and informal structures, commerce, and industry.

Protocol: A set of established guidelines for actions (which may be designated by individuals, teams, functions, or capabilities) under various specified conditions.

Public Information: Processes, procedures, and systems for communicating timely, accurate, and accessible information on an incident's cause, size, and current situation; resources committed; and other matters of general interest to the public, responders, and additional stakeholders (both directly affected and indirectly affected).

Public Information Officer: A member of the Command Staff responsible for interfacing with the public and media and/or with other agencies with incident-related information requirements.

Publications Management: Subsystem that manages the development, publication control, publication supply, and distribution of *National Incident Management System* materials.

Recovery: The development, coordination, and execution of service- and site-restoration plans; the reconstitution of government operations and services; individual, private-sector, nongovernmental, and public assistance programs to provide housing and to promote restoration; long-term care and treatment of affected persons; additional measures for social, political, environmental, and economic restoration; evaluation of the incident to identify lessons learned; postincident reporting; and development of initiatives to mitigate the effects of future incidents.

Recovery Plan: A plan developed to restore an affected area or community.

Reimbursement: A mechanism to recoup funds expended for incident-specific activities.

Resource Management: A system for identifying available resources at all jurisdictional levels to enable timely, efficient, and unimpeded access to resources needed to prepare for, respond to, or recover from an incident. Resource management under the *National Incident Management System* includes mutual aid agreements and assistance agreements; the use of special Federal, State, tribal, and local teams; and resource mobilization protocols.

Resource Tracking: A standardized, integrated process conducted prior to, during, and after an incident by all emergency management/response personnel and their associated organizations.

Resources: Personnel and major items of equipment, supplies, and facilities available or potentially available for assignment to incident operations and for which status is maintained. Resources are described by kind and type and may be used in operational support or supervisory capacities at an incident or at an Emergency Operations Center.

Response: Activities that address the short-term, direct effects of an incident. Response includes immediate actions to save lives, protect property, and meet basic human needs. Response also includes the execution of emergency operations plans and of mitigation activities designed to limit the loss of life, personal injury, property damage, and other unfavorable outcomes. As indicated by the situation, response activities include applying intelligence and other information to lessen the effects or consequences of an incident; increased security operations; continuing investigations into nature and source of the threat; ongoing public health and agricultural surveillance and testing processes; immunizations, isolation, or quarantine; and specific law enforcement operations aimed at preempting, interdicting, or disrupting illegal activity, and apprehending actual perpetrators and bringing them to justice.

Retrograde: To return resources back to their original location.

Safety Officer: A member of the Command Staff responsible for monitoring incident operations and advising the Incident Commander on all matters relating to operational safety, including the health and safety of emergency responder personnel.

Section: The Incident Command System organizational level having responsibility for a major functional area of incident management (e.g., Operations, Planning, Logistics, Finance/Administration, and Intelligence/Investigations (if established)). The Section is organizationally situated between the Branch and the Incident Command.

Single Resource: An individual, a piece of equipment and its personnel complement, or a crew/team of individuals with an identified work supervisor that can be used on an incident.

Situation Report: Confirmed or verified information regarding the specific details relating to an incident.

Span of Control: The number of resources for which a supervisor is responsible, usually expressed as the ratio of supervisors to individuals. Under the *National Incident Management System*, an appropriate span of control is between 1:3 and 1:7, with optimal being 1:5, or between 1:8 and 1:10 for many large-scale law enforcement operations.

Special Needs Population: A population whose members may have additional needs before, during, and after an incident in functional areas, including but not limited to: maintaining independence, communication, transportation, supervision, and medical care. Individuals in need of additional response assistance may include those who have disabilities; who live in institutionalized settings; who are elderly; who are children; who are from diverse cultures, who have limited English proficiency, or who are non-English-speaking; or who are transportation disadvantaged.

Staging Area: Temporary location for available resources. A Staging Area can be any location in which personnel, supplies, and equipment can be temporarily housed or parked while awaiting operational assignment.

Standard Operating Guidelines: A set of instructions having the force of a directive, covering those features of operations which lend themselves to a definite or standardized procedure without loss of effectiveness.

Standard Operating Procedure: A complete reference document or an operations manual that provides the purpose, authorities, duration, and details for the preferred method of performing a single function or a number of interrelated functions in a uniform manner.

State: When capitalized, refers to any State of the United States, the District of Columbia, the Commonwealth of Puerto Rico, the Virgin Islands, Guam, American Samoa, the Commonwealth of the Northern Mariana Islands, and any possession of the United States. See Section 2 (14), Homeland Security Act of 2002, Pub. L. 107-296, 116 Stat. 2135 (2002).

Status Report: Information specifically related to the status of resources (e.g., the availability or assignment of resources).

Strategy: The general plan or direction selected to accomplish incident objectives.

Strike Team: A set number of resources of the same kind and type that have an established minimum number of personnel, common communications, and a leader.

Substate Region: A grouping of jurisdictions, counties, and/or localities within a State brought together for specified purposes (e.g., homeland security, education, public health), usually containing a governance structure.

Supervisor: The Incident Command System title for an individual responsible for a Division or Group.

Supporting Agency: An agency that provides support and/or resource assistance to another agency. See **Assisting Agency**.

Supporting Technology: Any technology that may be used to support the *National Incident Management System*, such as orthophoto mapping, remote automatic weather stations, infrared technology, or communications.

System: Any combination of facilities, equipment, personnel, processes, procedures, and communications integrated for a specific purpose.

Tactics: The deployment and directing of resources on an incident to accomplish the objectives designated by strategy.

Task Force: Any combination of resources assembled to support a specific mission or operational need. All resource elements within a Task Force must have common communications and a designated leader.

Technical Specialist: Person with special skills that can be used anywhere within the Incident Command System organization. No minimum qualifications are prescribed, as technical specialists normally perform the same duties during an incident that they perform in their everyday jobs, and they are typically certified in their fields or professions.

Technology Standards: Conditions, guidelines, or characteristics that may be required to facilitate the interoperability and compatibility of major systems across jurisdictional, geographic, and functional lines.

Technology Support: Assistance that facilitates incident operations and sustains the research and development programs that underpin the long-term investment in the Nation's future incident management capabilities.

Terrorism: As defined in the Homeland Security Act of 2002, activity that involves an act that is dangerous to human life or potentially destructive of critical infrastructure or key resources; is a violation of the criminal laws of the United States or of any State or other subdivision of the United States; and appears to be intended to intimidate or coerce a civilian population, to influence the policy of a government by intimidation or coercion, or to affect the conduct of a government by mass destruction, assassination, or kidnapping.

Threat: Natural or manmade occurrence, individual, entity, or action that has or indicates the potential to harm life, information, operations, the environment, and/or property.

Tools: Those instruments and capabilities that allow for the professional performance of tasks, such as information systems, agreements, doctrine, capabilities, and legislative authorities.

Tribal: Referring to any Indian tribe, band, nation, or other organized group or community, including any Alaskan Native Village as defined in or established pursuant to the Alaskan Native Claims Settlement Act (85 Stat. 688) [43 U.S.C.A. and 1601 et seq.], that is recognized as eligible for the special programs and services provided by the United States to Indians because of their status as Indians.

Type: An Incident Command System resource classification that refers to capability. Type 1 is generally considered to be more capable than Types 2, 3, or 4, respectively, because of size, power, capacity, or (in the case of Incident Management Teams) experience and qualifications.

Unified Approach: The integration of resource management, communications and information management, and command and management in order to form an effective system.

Unified Area Command: Version of command established when incidents under an Area Command are multijurisdictional. See **Area Command**.

Unified Command (UC): An Incident Command System application used when more than one agency has incident jurisdiction or when incidents cross political jurisdictions. Agencies work together through the designated members of the UC, often the senior persons from agencies and/or disciplines participating in the UC, to establish a common set of objectives and strategies and a single Incident Action Plan.

Unit: The organizational element with functional responsibility for a specific incident planning, logistics, or finance/administration activity.

Unit Leader: The individual in charge of managing Units within an Incident Command System (ICS) functional Section. The Unit can be staffed by a number of support personnel providing a wide range of services. Some of the support positions are preestablished within ICS (e.g., Base/Camp Manager), but many others will be assigned as technical specialists.

Unity of Command: An Incident Command System principle stating that each individual involved in incident operations will be assigned to only one supervisor.

Vital Records: The essential agency records that are needed to meet operational responsibilities under national security emergencies or other emergency or disaster conditions (emergency operating records), or to protect the legal and financial rights of the government and those affected by government activities (legal and financial rights records).

Volunteer: For purposes of the *National Incident Management System*, any individual accepted to perform services by the lead agency (which has authority to accept volunteer services) when the individual performs services without promise, expectation, or receipt of compensation for services performed. See 16 U.S.C. 742f(c) and 29 CFR 553.101.

ACRONYMS

CIKR	Critical Infrastructure and Key Resources
CPG	Comprehensive Preparedness Guide
DHS	Department of Homeland Security
DOC	Department Operations Center
EMAC	Emergency Management Assistance Compact
EMS	Emergency Medical Services
EMT	Emergency Medical Technician
EOC	Emergency Operations Center
HAZMAT	Hazardous Material
HSPD-5	Homeland Security Presidential Directive 5, "Management of Domestic Incidents"
HSPD-7	Homeland Security Presidential Directive 7, "Critical Infrastructure Identification, Prioritization, and Protection"
HSPD-8	Homeland Security Presidential Directive 8, "National Preparedness"
IAP	Incident Action Plan
IC	Incident Commander
ICP	Incident Command Post
ICS	Incident Command System
IMT	Incident Management Team
IPS	Integrated Planning System
JIC	Joint Information Center
JIS	Joint Information System
MAC	Multiagency Coordination
MACS	Multiagency Coordination System
NFPA	National Fire Protection Association
NGO	Nongovernmental Organization
NIC	National Integration Center
NIMS	*National Incident Management System*
NIPP	*National Infrastructure Protection Plan*
NRF	*National Response Framework*
NSPD	National Security Presidential Directive
R&D	Research and Development
SDO	Standards Development Organization
SOP	Standard Operating Procedure
TCL	Target Capabilities List
UC	Unified Command

INDEX

INDEX